WHAT YOU MEANT, WHAT I HEARD

How Perspective Shapes Connection, Conflict &
the Meaning of Every Moment

Dustin Garr

Printed in the United States of America.
First Edition.

ISBN: 979-8-9949070-1-6
Cover design: Samuel A.

The insights in this book are drawn from the author's own experiences and reflections. Certain events have been adapted, expanded, or fictionalized for clarity, privacy, or illustrative purposes. These stories are crafted to teach, not to document. This book is not intended to provide professional psychological, legal, or therapeutic guidance.

For the people who have shaped me—through clarity, through confusion, through love, through growth.

For anyone who has ever wished to understand others and be understood themselves.

And finally, for my wife, whose steady love, honesty, and strength have shown me what true understanding feels like.

Table of Contents

What You Meant, What I Heard

There are moments in life where you feel like you're speaking clearly—clear intentions, clear words, clear meaning—yet somehow the other person walks away with an entirely different message. It's a frustrating experience. You walk away thinking, "How did that get misunderstood? How did my meaning get lost? What did I say wrong?"

But ask the other person, and they're equally confused. "I heard exactly what you said," they think. "How else was I supposed to interpret it?"

That gap—between what you meant and what they heard—is where misunderstanding grows, where frustration lives, where unnecessary conflict thrives, and where relationships, teams, and trust quietly fall apart.

Most people assume communication breaks because someone said the wrong thing, used the wrong tone, or chose the wrong words. But after years of leading people, building businesses, working with family, resolving conflicts, sitting across from clients, raising kids, and trying to navigate my own relationships, I began to realize something:

Words aren't the problem. Perspective is.

What people hear has far more to do with what they believe, fear, expect, or assume than the actual words spoken. What you meant gets filtered through their experiences, insecurities, hopes, disappointments, and history.

Your words enter someone else's world—and that world changes everything.

At first, this realization frustrated me. I didn't want to have to account for someone else's perspective. I wanted people to just hear me. I wanted my intentions to be enough. But intentions don't travel well without perspective. Meaning gets bent. Tone gets magnified. Emotion gets assumed. And clarity gets lost.

The longer I lived, and the more leadership and personal experiences I gathered, the clearer it became: Communication isn't just what you say—it's what the other person is capable of hearing.

This book was born from that discovery.

For years, I've watched people talk past each other at work, at home, in friendships, and in marriages. I've watched small misunderstandings grow into giant fractures. I've watched people assume offense where none existed, assume motives that weren't true, and assume emotions that weren't intended. I've watched simple disagreements become full-blown conflict because someone saw the situation from a different angle.

And behind almost every one of those breakdowns was not a lack of intelligence, effort, or care but a lack of *perspective*—not seeing the deeper currents beneath the surface.

When you understand perspective—your own and others'—something powerful happens:

You begin to hear the real message beneath the words.
You begin to see the tension beneath the reaction.
You begin to understand the reason behind the emotion.
You begin to notice what people are afraid to say.

You begin to understand people, truly understand them, in a way you never could before.

Perspective changes everything.

This book is designed to help you see what's really happening beneath your conversations, conflicts, disappointments, and daily interactions. To help you pause long enough to ask questions you've never thought to ask. To help you slow down long enough to see the seam between your world and someone else's.

Because that seam—that thin line where two perspectives meet—is where understanding happens.

It's where connection grows.
It's where trust is built.
It's where clarity begins.

My goal is simple:
To help you see differently so you can live differently.
To help you understand others so you can connect more deeply.
To help you recognize the invisible currents shaping your

relationships so you can navigate   them with wisdom instead of frustration.

Communication isn't magic; it's a skill.
Perspective isn't luck; it's a tool.
Understanding isn't automatic; it's intentional.

This book doesn't promise to fix everything overnight —no book can—but it will equip you with the tools to start building trust, strengthening relationships, navigating conflict, and transforming the way you hear, speak, lead, and love.

You don't need perfect communication. You need better perspective.

Acknowledgements

To the people who taught me perspective long before I knew the word for it—thank you.

To the misunderstandings that humbled me and the clarity that rebuilt me—thank you.

To the friends, mentors, and family members who sharpened my thinking, challenged my angles, and showed me what it means to be understood—thank you.

To every reader who chooses growth over comfort, honesty over convenience, and clarity over assumption—this book is for you.

INTRODUCTION

Why This Book Exists

Every day, people misinterpret each other without realizing it.

Not because they're careless.
Not because they don't care.
But because most people have never been taught how to see themselves clearly or each other.

Life gets easier when you learn to interpret moments, emotions, and people accurately.

Relationships grow deeper.
Conflict becomes manageable.
Communication becomes honest instead of defensive.
Identity becomes grounded instead of reactive.
And you move through the world with more steadiness and confidence.

This book is built on a simple belief:

Clarity is not complicated; but it's not automatic, either. It must be practiced.

Clarity means you can see what's actually happening—inside you and around you—before you respond.

This book exists because clarity is not automatic.

It's a skill. And like any skill, it must be practiced.

Throughout these chapters, you'll learn how to:

- widen your emotional horizon
- understand your own reactions
- interpret others more generously
- stay steady during conflict
- strengthen your identity
- reframe your past
- build a clearer future

If you ever wished conversations were easier…
If you ever wished connections felt safer…
If you ever wished you could stop misreading the people you love…
If you ever wished life made more sense…

This book was written for you.

As you read, you'll see yourself in these pages.

This isn't a book you read once. This is a book you live with.

Because clarity doesn't just change how you understand moments—it changes how you live your life.

And that's where perspective becomes power.

Let's begin.

PART I
SEEING CLEARLY

THE CURRENT YOU DON'T SEE

How to Notice What Others Miss

Most people think they're seeing the whole picture. They aren't.

They're standing in the same river, under the same conditions, with the same information—yet missing what actually matters. Not because it's hidden, but because it's subtle and requires a trained eye. Because perspective determines what you notice.

In life, just like in water, the most important currents are rarely obvious. They don't announce themselves. They don't splash. They sit quietly beneath the surface, shaping outcomes for those who know how to read them—and frustrating those who don't.

This chapter is about learning to see what others overlook. The seams beneath conversations. The emotional currents beneath reactions. The invisible forces shaping how people respond, connect, and misunderstand each other.

The difference between clarity and confusion isn't effort; it's perspective.

And once you learn to see the current, everything changes.

RESULTS CHANGE THE MOMENT PERCEPTION CHANGES

Most people think water is water. That a river is a river and a current is a current. You stand in it, you cast into it, and you hope something bites.

But if you've ever fished with someone who truly understands water—someone who can read current the way most people read a map—you know that's not how it works at all.

There's a deeper level to everything.

I was waist-deep in the Provo River with my uncle, someone who had fished those waters long enough to understand their hidden language. The mist hovered low, creating that early-evening blur where sky and river trade soft borders. The light was fading. The air had that quiet calm that always seems to settle over water right before dusk.

My uncle stood about ten feet away, almost shoulder to shoulder with me. Same water. Same conditions. Same gear. Same fly.

But he was catching fish, and I wasn't.

Cast after cast, I watched him lift his rod, feel the subtle resistance, and bring in another trout. I wasn't just behind—I was completely missing something.

"Okay," I finally said, half-laughing, half-frustrated. "What are you doing differently?"

He didn't look over. He just kept false-casting, keeping his line high. "Nothing," he said casually. "You're just not seeing what I see."

I scanned the river again—clear, glassy, moving steadily. Nothing unusual. No magic. No secret doorway.

"What do you see?" I asked.

He nodded toward a faint ripple line. "Right there," he said. "Where the bubbles flatten out. That's a seam. Two currents meeting. Fish sit right on the edge. Not in the fast water—too much energy. Not in the slow— not enough flow. Right *there*. That overlap. Cast along it, not into it."

I looked. At first, I saw nothing. Then slowly the texture changed in front of me. What looked like one current revealed itself as several. The water wasn't uniform—it was layered, shifting, intersecting. The seam was subtle but unmistakable once you knew what to look for.

While my uncle had a great time gloating in his success, I'd been throwing my fly straight into the fast flow—the worst place to cast if you actually want to catch something.

Same river. Same gear. Same fly. Different results.

Why? He saw something I didn't.

He had perspective.

PERSPECTIVE CHANGES WHAT YOU NOTICE

That day taught me something that has shaped every relationship, leadership moment, conflict, and conversation I've had since.

Two people can be in the same situation, at the same time, with the same information—and still see completely different things.

One person sees intention; another sees threat. One person sees opportunity; another sees risk. One sees effort; another sees failure. One sees kindness; another sees obligation. One sees directness; another sees aggression.

Two people, same moment, but totally different experiences. The difference isn't in what happened, it's in what each person *sees*.

Your perspective is the lens that determines what feels true. What matters. What hurts. What helps. What offends. What motivates.

Perspective shapes everything.

Most conflicts don't come from what happened, they come from the different meanings each person attaches to what happened.

The Invisible Lens

Everyone carries a lens made from:

- childhood experiences
- past wounds
- victories and failures
- beliefs
- expectations
- insecurities
- personality
- current emotional state

This lens determines what you notice, what you assume, and what you believe someone else meant.

It determines how you read tone. How you interpret silence and assign meaning to someone's actions. How you evaluate fairness, respect, responsibility, and effort.

You don't see "the truth." You see "your version of the truth."

Just like I didn't see the seam—even though it was right in front of me—people don't see each other's intentions. They don't see each other's fears. They don't see each other's history. They only see the river from their angle.

Perspective is invisible unless someone points it out—and even then, it takes time to learn to see it.

THE COST OF MISSING THE SEAM

In fishing, missing the seam means you won't catch fish. In relationships, missing the seam means you won't catch understanding.

If you don't understand where someone is coming from, you'll misread what they mean. You'll fill in the blanks with assumptions. You'll react to your perception instead of responding to their reality.

And that's where misunderstandings grow. Not in what was said but in the seam between what was meant and what was heard.

Learning to see the seam in communication—that intersection of two different emotional currents—is one of the most powerful skills you can develop.

LEARNING TO READ THE RIVER OF PEOPLE

Just like water, people have currents.

Fast currents of stress. Slow currents of fatigue. Deep currents of insecurity. Shallow currents of distraction. Turbulent currents of fear. Steady currents of confidence.

In the same vein, every conversation has layers beneath the surface. Every reaction has a source beneath the emotion. Every misunderstanding has a current beneath the words.

The better you get at reading people's currents, the easier it becomes to navigate them.

Perspective is the difference between:

- reacting and understanding
- assuming and noticing
- judging and empathizing
- exploding and responding
- frustration and clarity

Reading water is no different than learning to read someone's emotional state. In both cases, the skill is the same:

Seeing what others miss. Noticing what others overlook. Understanding what others react to. Seeing the deeper current beneath the surface.

And when you do, your relationships, leadership, connection, and communication transform.

CHAPTER 2

HEARING BEYOND WORDS

How to Listen for Meaning, Not Just Message

Words are simple. Meaning is not.

Most people believe they are clear communicators. They believe they "say what they mean." But meaning isn't carried in words alone—it's carried in context, tone, timing, emotion, history, and unspoken expectation.

You've probably had moments where someone said something small— a light comment, a short question, a simple statement—and you reacted more strongly than the situation seemed to deserve.

Was it the words? Or the meaning you heard behind them?

Meaning doesn't travel neutrally; it gets filtered. And the biggest filter of all is perspective.

This chapter will help you learn to listen and understand the meaning behind what is being said.

THE HOMEOWNER

Years ago, I was working on a custom home for a woman who had strong opinions about nearly every detail. She cared deeply about the project, and I respected that. But no matter how much effort we put in, no matter how many times I thought I'd given her exactly what she asked for, she always came back with stress, worry, or frustration.

One day she called, anxious and irritated.

"Dustin, the paint color isn't right," she said.

I looked at it—it was exactly what was selected.

"It matches the sample," I told her confidently.

"That's not what I meant!" she countered, exasperated.

And I remember thinking, *"How can the color not be what she meant if we used the exact color she chose?"*

Her tone escalated. She began listing more things:

- "The kitchen isn't how I pictured it."
- "The tile looks colder than I expected."
- "The lighting feels off."
- "The bedroom doesn't feel cozy."

Everything she described wasn't about the *items*—it was about the *feeling* she expected those items to create.

She wasn't looking at the paint swatch. She was looking at a picture in her mind.

It finally hit me. I was building her house; she was building her home.

Two completely different projects.

I was hearing words through the lens of tasks, budgets, and measurable decisions. She, on the other hand, was speaking through the lens of meaning, emotion, and lived experience.

When I said, "It matches the sample," she didn't hear reassurance. She heard, "Stop complaining. You picked this." When she said, "That's not what I meant," what she actually meant was, "I'm scared this won't feel like home."

Her fear wasn't the color. Her fear was ending up with something she didn't love.

WHAT YOU HEAR DEPENDS ON WHAT YOU'RE LISTENING FOR

Most people don't listen for meaning—they listen for information.

They listen to respond. To solve. To win. To defend. To explain. To correct. To clarify.

But listening for meaning is different.

Listening for meaning requires you to set aside your assumptions long enough to truly understand what someone is trying to say—not just the words they chose in the moment.

Words are imperfect tools. People rarely say what they actually mean. Most people don't even know what they mean until they feel safe enough to express it.

Listening for meaning means paying attention to:

- tone
- tension
- breathing
- pace
- body language
- emotional charge
- what the person repeats
- what they avoid
- what they emphasize

Every conversation has layers: The words spoken, the meaning intended, the fear underneath, and the hope beneath that.

The deeper you listen, the more clearly you understand the person behind the words.

THE THREE R'S OF TRUE LISTENING

Over time, I developed a simple tool to enhance true listening:

1. Receive

Don't interrupt. Don't problem-solve. Don't prepare your response.

Just receive the message fully. Let it land before you interpret it.

2. Reflect

Say back what you heard—not to parrot, but to confirm.

"So what you're feeling is…"

"So what you meant was…"

"You're saying that…"

Reflection reveals misalignment instantly.

3. Redirect

Once the meaning is clear, move the conversation toward resolution.

Not fixing. Not arguing. Not defending. Just gently guiding it forward.

When you skip the first two steps, you end up solving the wrong problem or responding to the wrong message.

Listening is not an act of silence—it's an act of curiosity.

A STORY ABOUT PERSPECTIVE IN CONFLICT

I once had a project manager and a subcontractor almost blow up at each other over a delivery delay.

The project manager believed the subcontractor was being lazy. The subcontractor believed the project manager was being unrealistic. They weren't arguing about the delivery. They were arguing about the story they told themselves about the delivery.

The project manager heard disrespect. The subcontractor heard blame.

Actually, neither was happening.

Once we sat down and listened—not to the words, but to the meaning—everything shifted. The tension dissolved. The conflict wasn't personal; it was perceptual.

THE BETTER QUESTION

The key to transforming your relationships lies in one simple shift in focus.

Instead of asking: "What did they say?"

Ask, "What did they mean?"

SPEAKING SO THEY CAN SEE IT

How to Communicate with Clarity and Compassion

Most misunderstandings don't happen because people disagree. They happen because people see different pictures.

We assume our words are clear because they're clear to us. We assume our meaning is obvious because *we* can see it. But clarity doesn't live in your intent.

It lives in what the other person is able to visualize.

Communication rarely breaks down because words are wrong. It breaks down because the images don't match.

One person speaks from experience while another listens from uncertainty. One sees structure and the other sees chaos. One understands the destination while another is still trying to understand the map.

And until those pictures align, understanding remains just out of reach.

This is something every builder knows well.

There's a moment on nearly every jobsite when a client stands inside a half-framed home—bare studs, open ceilings, exposed wires and plumbing—and says, "I'm trying to imagine how this is supposed to look."

You can see it on their face. They're trying… but they can't see it yet. You both are standing in the same space, looking at the same structure, but seeing two completely different realities.

You're seeing the finished product; they're seeing confusion. You see walls taking shape; they see missing answers. You see decades of experience; they feel uncertainty and risk.

It's not because they're ungrateful or incapable; it's because visualization is a learned skill.

Builders spend years learning how to see a finished home long before drywall, paint, and trim ever appear. Clients don't have that background. They're stepping into a world they've never navigated before.

And here's the key:

Communication works the exact same way.

Most people cannot visualize what you're saying unless you speak in a way they can see.

We assume others understand because *we* understand. We assume others visualize what we mean because we visualize it.

We assume our clarity transfers automatically.

But it doesn't.

Clarity in your mind is invisible to everyone else. If someone can't see what you're saying, they can't fully follow you. They can't trust you. They can't connect with you or grasp your intention.

Because clarity is not what you say—it's what the other person sees *because* of what you said.

This chapter is about closing that gap.

It's about learning how to speak in a way that helps others *see* what you mean—not just hear or receive it, but truly understand it.

Why is this important?

It's because people don't follow explanations. They follow clarity.

When someone can visualize your meaning:

- defensiveness softens
- trust increases
- confusion fades
- alignment becomes possible

That's when communication shifts from effort to connection.

Clarity is not saying more. It's saying what helps the other person see.

In this chapter, you'll learn how to:

- recognize when someone can't yet see what you mean,
- translate your understanding into something visual and relatable,
- bridge emotional and interpretive gaps with compassion,
- and speak in a way that invites understanding instead of resistance.

Because the goal of communication isn't to be right—it's to be understood. And understanding only happens when someone can finally see what you've been trying to say.

THE CUSTOM HOME JOBSITE

Years ago, I met a family at a jobsite to walk through their home mid-construction. The husband was excited and optimistic; the wife was quiet and hesitant. As we walked through the frame, the husband could "see it"—the rooms, the layout, the flow. His mind made the leap instantly.

But the wife struggled. She kept pausing. Looking around. Squinting into open spaces. She'd nod like she was trying to convince herself she understood, but I could sense the worry.

Finally, she turned to me and said, "It feels smaller than I thought."

This is something every builder hears at some point. Framing always feels small—until drywall goes up, until finish carpentry adds definition, until paint and flooring ground the space.

"What part feels small?" I asked gently.

She waved her hand around. "I don't know. All of it. I just can't picture it."

There it was—the seam between what I saw and what she saw.

I walked her into the kitchen area.

"Picture this," I said, pointing. "Your island is here. Sink here. Range here. The windows will be larger—this is just the framing. Your cabinets will pull the room wider visually. And the ceiling height will feel taller once drywall is in."

She nodded slowly, tension easing. "Oh…okay. Yes. That helps."

Did anything change about the room? Not at all.

The only thing that changed was her ability to visualize it—and that changed everything.

PEOPLE DON'T FOLLOW WORDS — THEY FOLLOW IMAGES

Your mind doesn't store words. It stores pictures.

When someone tells you about their childhood home, you don't remember the literal words—you imagine a scene. When someone tells you a fear, you create an emotional image. When someone tells you a dream, you see a possibility.

So if you want someone to understand you, you have to paint the picture for them.

People need:

- context
- imagery
- detail
- relatable examples
- emotional anchors

They need the *feeling* behind the words, not just the words.

THE CLARITY GAP

Every conversation has a hidden distance between what you mean and what the other person sees. Let's call that distance the clarity gap.

Some people speak in blueprints—structured, direct, logical, linear. Some people speak in color—emotional, intuitive, expressive. Some people speak in story—narrative, metaphor, image-driven. Some people speak in data—facts, timelines, steps, details.

When you communicate in a way that doesn't match how someone visualizes meaning, the clarity gap grows.

That gap creates:

- frustration
- confusion
- assumptions
- misinterpretations
- emotional reactions

Not because either person is wrong but because they picture differently.

YOUR JOB AS A COMMUNICATOR

Your job is not to be precise; it's to be *understandable.*

Your job is not to be perfect; it's to be *visual.*

Your job is not to speak more; it's to speak *clearer.*

And "clearer" doesn't always mean fewer words. Sometimes clarity requires *more* detail. More connection, more anchoring, more imagery. You have to help people see what you mean.

THE CLARITY CHECKLIST

Before any important conversation, ask yourself:

1. What am I trying to help them see? If you can't answer this clearly, you're not ready to speak.
2. What picture do I need to paint? What would help them visualize the meaning behind my words?
3. What context are they missing? Assumed knowledge is the enemy of clarity.
4. What emotion do I need to acknowledge? People won't hear your meaning if they feel unseen.
5. What outcome do I hope they walk away with? Clarity without direction just dumps more information on someone.

A STORY ABOUT MISCOMMUNICATION IN MARRIAGE

One morning, I was rushing to get out the door for a meeting. I grabbed my toast, grabbed my laptop, and called to my wife, "Hey, the dishwasher needs to be unloaded."

In my mind, I was simply communicating a task that needed attention today. In her mind, the sentence landed differently.

What she heard was: "You're not doing enough." What she felt was: "He's frustrated with me."

She didn't hear a task. She heard a tone.

That tone wasn't in my words—it was in the picture she saw based on her stress, her morning, and her emotional lens at that moment. We talked later, and I explained what I meant. We laughed about it.

But it taught me something important: People hear your words through the story they're already living. And that story shapes their visualization of your meaning.

If you don't help people see the right picture, they paint their own—often inaccurately.

SPEAK WITH VISION

Your words should build a picture clear enough that others can stand inside it.

Just like walking clients through a home being built, your communication must guide someone from confusion to clarity—not by giving them more words, but by giving them something to visualize.

When people can see what you mean, understanding follows. Trust, connection, and alignment follow.

THE QUESTION THAT CHANGES CONVERSATIONS

Before you speak, ask, "If I were in their situation, what would I need to see to understand me?"

That one question can shift your entire communication style. Communication isn't about speaking your truth—it's about helping someone else see it.

THE ANGLE OF UNDERSTANDING

One Wall, Two Truths

Every builder knows this simple, frustrating truth:

A wall can be perfectly straight and still look crooked—depending on where you stand.

You put a level on it, check the plumb, square the corners, run your tape from end to end…everything reads true. But take three steps to the left, or shift where the sun hits the sheetrock, and suddenly your eyes swear the wall is leaning.

Nothing changed about the wall. Everything changed about the angle.

People are no different.

Two people can look at the exact same moment—the same sentence, the same tone, the same facial expression—and walk away with two completely different interpretations. Not because someone is lying or wrong, but because they're standing in different emotional positions.

Perspective isn't about right or wrong.

Perspective is about where you're standing when you look.

THE CROOKED WALL THAT WASN'T CROOKED

There was a home we built where the homeowner stood in the hallway staring at a wall like it had personally offended him. Arms folded. Brow tight. Head tilting like he was lining up a pool shot.

"This wall is off," he said. "I can see it from here."

I'd heard this before. And if you've been in construction long enough, you start to know that what a person *sees* and what a level *says* are not always the same thing.

We checked everything anyway:

- framing: perfect
- level: perfect
- measurements: spot on

But from where he stood—literally and emotionally—the wall really did look bowed.

Why?

Because he was standing at the exact angle where the afternoon light caught the texture just right, casting a shadow that made the surface appear to dip inward.

The wall wasn't crooked. The lighting and the angle created the illusion.

So I walked him to the opposite end of the hall, lined up his sightline with the studs, and had him look again.

His face changed instantly.

"Oh…" he said, almost embarrassed. "Now it looks straight." He laughed. "That's wild. Totally different view."

Nothing had changed about the wall.

His truth shifted because his perspective shifted.

TWO PEOPLE, SAME WALL, DIFFERENT TRUTHS

That moment has stuck with me for years because it's exactly how relationships work.

One person stands at an angle shaped by stress, exhaustion, old wounds, or assumptions. The other stands at a different angle shaped by logic, optimism, calm, or distance.

Same situation.

Same facts.

Same conversation.

But they're catching different shadows.

And so each one sees something *real* from where they're standing—a truth shaped by angle, light, and experience.

Most conflicts aren't about facts. They're about **angles**.

Once you learn to walk around the wall—to step into the other person's position, to borrow their view for a moment—the whole picture changes.

And more often than not, **you discover the wall was straight all along.**

EMOTION CREATES ANGLES

Just like light creates shadows on a wall, **emotion creates angles in your perception.** You never look at a situation from a neutral point of view—you look from where your emotions position you.

Each emotion tilts your perspective in a different way:

- **Stress creates a downward angle:** Everything feels heavier, sharper, more urgent than it actually is. Small issues look like big ones.
- **Fear creates a narrowing angle:** You stop seeing options and start seeing threats. Every tone feels loaded, every pause feels intentional.
- **Fatigue creates a distorted angle:** Clarity bends. Objectivity wobbles. You misread signals simply because you're out of emotional energy.
- **Insecurity creates a hyper-sensitive angle:** A neutral comment sounds like criticism. A simple request feels like rejection.
- **Pride creates a blind spot:** You see the flaws in others clearly, but not the part you're playing. Pride blocks perspective as effectively as standing too close to the wall.
- **Assumption creates a tunnel:** You stop being curious. You stop listening. You interpret everything through the story you already decided was true.

- **Hope creates an idealized angle:** You see potential more than reality. You overlook red flags and fill in the gaps with what you *want* to be there.
- **Past hurt creates a defensive angle:** Your guard goes up before the conversation even begins. You expect pain, so you prepare for it—even when none is coming.

Emotions don't just influence how you feel. They bend the angle from which you see. Your emotional state becomes the position you're standing in—your vantage point, your height, your lighting, your shadows.

That's why two days can feel completely different even when the situation hasn't changed. Your angle changed.

That's why a comment that didn't bother you last week can offend you today. Your angle shifted.

That's why some conflicts melt away after sleep, a walk or a meal. Your angle reset.

You never see a situation with pure objectivity; you always see through the emotional angle you're standing in at that moment.

And once you understand the angle, you understand your reaction. Once you understand your reaction, you can finally adjust your response. And that angle—that tiny shift—changes everything.

YOU REACT TO WHAT YOU SEE FROM WHERE YOU STAND

Every reaction you have is shaped by the emotional position you're standing in. Not by the moment itself—but by the *angle* you're looking from.

If someone snaps at you unexpectedly, the moment is the same for everyone involved. But your *angle* determines your interpretation:

- **If your angle is insecurity:** *"They must be mad at me."* You assume you triggered something. You brace for impact.
- **If your angle is confidence:** *"They must be having a rough day."* You give space instead of taking offense.

- **If your angle is fear:** *"What did I do wrong?"* You scan for mistakes, preparing for rejection.
- **If your angle is peace:** *"That reaction probably isn't about me."* You stay steady because you know other people have storms too.
- **If your angle is exhaustion:** *"I can't deal with this right now."* Everything feels heavier, even small moments.
- **If your angle is past hurt:** *"Here we go again..."* Old wounds step into the present and color the moment.
- **If your angle is trust:** *"Something must be off—I'll check on them."* You move toward connection rather than defensiveness.

Same tone. Same moment. Same behavior from the other person.

Different emotional footing → different interpretation → different reaction.

That's why perspective matters so much.

Two people can stand in the same conversation and walk away with completely different realities—not because of the words, but because of the angle through which those words were filtered.

The moment doesn't define your reaction. Your angle does.

And once you understand this, everything changes:

You stop assuming the worst, start looking for the angle, react less spontaneously, and understand more.

This is because the goal isn't to correct the moment —it's to check the angle you're bringing into it.

YOUR ANGLE IS INVISIBLE TO YOU

Here's what makes perspective so difficult to recognize in the moment:

Your angle feels like the truth.

When you're looking at a wall, you don't think, "Ah, this is just the angle I happen to be standing at." You think, "The wall is crooked."

The same thing happens emotionally.

You don't say to yourself, "This is my current emotional lens speaking."

You say, "This is what's happening."

Your brain presents your interpretation as reality   not as a guess, not as a possibility, but as the truth. That's why two people can stand in the same moment and swear they experienced two different realities.

Your angle feels natural to you because:

- you've lived inside it for years
- it's shaped by your history, beliefs, fears, and expectations
- it matches the stories you've learned to trust
- it confirms what you were already primed to see
- it sits so close to you that you mistake it for objectivity

What you think is happening and what is actually happening are often two completely different things—separated not by facts, but by your angle.

If you've ever looked back on a moment and thought, "Maybe I overreacted…" or "Maybe that wasn't what they meant…" or "I might have seen that wrong…" then you've already experienced this split.

Your emotional position—your distance, your lighting, your shadows, your old stories—creates an invisible filter. And unless you slow down, reflect, or change your vantage point, that filter becomes your reality.

The challenge isn't that we have angles. Everyone does.

The challenge is that our own angle is the hardest one to see.

Only when you're willing to question it—to step two feet to the left, adjust the lighting, or look from someone else's position—do you start to realize you weren't seeing the moment incorrectly.

You were just seeing it incompletely.

A CONFLICT BETWEEN BROTHERS

Two brothers were building a business together, and over time the tension around finances kept rising like pressure behind a dam.

It started small—missed details, unclear updates, uneven expectations—but eventually every conversation felt heavier than it should have. One brother became convinced the other was hiding information while the other felt constantly interrogated and unfairly judged.

Neither belief was accurate.

But both beliefs felt real.

That's what emotional angles do: They turn ordinary moments into meaningful ones, even when nothing significant happened.

To understand the brothers' conflict, you have to understand their angles.

The older brother's angle:

"I've always had to be responsible. If I don't stay on top of things, everything falls apart."

Responsibility wasn't just a value for him—it was an identity he'd carried since childhood.

The younger brother's angle:

"People rarely trust me. I always have to prove myself."

For him, even neutral questions felt like tests he was destined to fail.

When those two angles collided, everything in their business partnership became emotionally charged.

- A simple budgeting question sounded like criticism.
- A delayed text response felt like secrecy.
- A request for clarity came across as accusation.
- A differing opinion triggered old insecurities.

They weren't reacting to the spreadsheet or the numbers. They were reacting to the shadows behind them.

Nothing was wrong with their intentions. Nothing was wrong with their effort.

Everything was happening at the level of angle.

One day, during a conversation that felt like it was about to fall apart again, they paused. And instead of defending their positions, they walked—slowly—into each other's perspectives.

The older brother realized, "He's not being evasive…he's scared he'll be viewed as unreliable again."

The younger brother realized, "He's not interrogating me…he's terrified something will slip through the cracks and land on his shoulders."

Nothing changed about the financial situation. Nothing changed about the facts. What changed was the *angle.* And with that shift, the conflict dissolved—not because it was solved, but because it was finally understood.

This is the heart of perspective:

Understanding begins when you stop fighting someone's reaction and start exploring the angle behind it.

When you do, the whole conversation changes—from accusation to insight, from defensiveness to connection, from tension to teamwork.

THE FOUR DISTORTIONS OF PERSPECTIVE

Just like angles distort walls, **emotional angles** distort communication.

These distortions change not what was said, but *how it's interpreted.* They warp clarity the same way light, shadow, and distance can warp a straight wall.

Here are the four primary distortions you'll see throughout this book— the "optical illusions" of human connection.

1. Light Distortion

Stress changes how things look—even when nothing changed at all.

In construction, if light hits a wall at the wrong angle, it can make a perfectly smooth surface look wavy. The wall didn't move; the lighting did.

Communication works the exact same way.

When you're under stress, pressure, fatigue, or emotional overload, even a neutral comment can look like criticism. A small problem can appear much larger. A passing tone can feel like a personal attack.

Stress becomes the "harsh lighting" that exaggerates flaws, amplifies emotions, and makes everything look more dramatic than it actually is.

Light distortion makes moments look worse than they are.

It convinces you that the problem is bigger, the comment is sharper, and the intention is darker.

Most arguments that escalate quickly do so under the glare of emotional lighting—not actual conflict.

2. Distance Distortion

Too close and you lose clarity. Too far and you lose connection.

Stand too close to a wall and you'll see every tiny imperfection. Back up too far and you might miss the obvious.

Emotionally, the same distortion happens:

- **When you're too close**, you can't see clearly. You're emotionally invested, sensitive, protective, or already hurt. Every word feels personal. Every tone feels loaded. Perspective narrows.
- **When you're too far**, you lose empathy. You detach, minimize, dismiss, or withdraw. You see the situation but not the person. You observe but you don't feel.

Distance determines clarity.

Being too close distorts details. Being too far distorts meaning.

The goal isn't closeness or distance—it's alignment.
Enough closeness to care.
Enough distance to stay grounded.

3. Shadow Distortion

Old wounds cast long shadows over new conversations.

Just like shadows make a straight wall look bent, your past can make a neutral moment feel threatening.

Shadow distortion is when:

- A past betrayal makes you suspicious of present intentions.
- A childhood wound turns feedback into rejection.
- An old argument resurfaces in a new discussion.
- A tone you've heard before triggers a reaction you didn't expect.

Your mind connects the present moment with past pain—even when the two are unrelated.

This is why someone says, "Are you mad at me?" when nothing is wrong and a simple comment lands like a hit to the heart.

Shadow distortion isn't about what's happening. It's about what your history *reminds* you of.

People often react to old experiences, not current conversations. They're not responding to the moment—they're responding to the shadow behind it.

4. Angle Distortion

Your belief system creates a fixed viewpoint—even when another angle might be truer.

Some walls only look straight from the angle you're used to standing in. Move three feet, and you see something different.

Your personal angle is shaped by:

- upbringing
- core beliefs
- personality
- cultural expectations
- emotional wiring
- identity roles

This angle creates a predictable way of interpreting the world:

- If you expect criticism, you hear criticism.
- If you expect conflict, you prepare for conflict.
- If you expect disappointment, you assume it's coming.

Your angle becomes your default perspective—even when the situation doesn't fit that narrative.

Angle distortion locks you into one interpretation, even when multiple truths exist.

It's not wrong—it's just incomplete.

The challenge is learning to shift angles when the moment requires it.

WHY THESE DISTORTIONS MATTER

Each distortion creates a different version of the truth.

Not lies—interpretations.

They explain why two intelligent, caring people can walk away from the same moment convinced they witnessed different realities.

Understanding these distortions doesn't eliminate conflict. It gives you the tools to see it with clarity instead of confusion.

Once you understand how angles distort your perception, you stop defending your view and start exploring the view you haven't seen yet.

THE SHIFT THAT CHANGES EVERYTHING

There's a moment—right before misunderstanding becomes conflict—when everything tightens.

Your chest. Your tone. Your assumptions.

That split-second is where most relationships break down and where they can just as easily break open.

The simplest way to change it?

Ask two questions that shift your entire perspective:

"Where am I standing right now, emotionally?"

"Where are they standing?"

You're not asking for blame. You're not asking who's right. You're asking **from which angle** the moment is being seen.

And that shift—small, subtle, quiet—is often enough to soften your mind and steady your heart.

Because conflict is rarely about what happened. It's about **the angle you were standing in when it happened.**

Maybe you were standing in stress.
Maybe they were standing in insecurity.
Maybe you were standing in exhaustion.
Maybe they were standing in fear.
Maybe you were standing in old memories.
Maybe they were standing in pressure you didn't know about.

Two people. Same moment. Different emotional elevations, distances, shadows, and lighting.

Just like a wall that looks crooked from one corner and perfectly straight from another, a conversation can feel hostile from your angle and harmless from theirs.

Seeing that doesn't excuse poor behavior—but it **explains** the mismatch.

When you pause long enough to consider where each person is standing:

- tension loses its urgency,
- assumptions loosen their grip,
- and understanding becomes possible.

This is the shift that changes everything:

Move your feet before you move your mouth, check your angle before you check their attitude, and look for the position before you judge the intention.

When you change where you're standing emotionally, you change what you see. And often, that's all a conversation needs to find clarity again.

A LEADERSHIP EXAMPLE

A team once came to me with fire in their eyes and frustration in their voices.

They were upset—convinced another department "wasn't doing their job," "wasn't carrying their weight," and "kept slowing everything down."

You could feel the tension walking down the hallway with them. Their arms were crossed, their sentences were clipped, and their patience was clearly worn thin.

Before we went any further, I asked a simple question:

"Have you seen this from their angle?"

The whole group fell quiet. Not defensive. Just silent—because they realized they hadn't even tried.

We grabbed a conference room and pulled up the other team's workload—every deadline, every backlog item, every emergency request that had hit them in the last week. We looked at the staffing gaps they were managing, the pressure they were under from leadership, the projects they were supporting that no one else ever saw, and the actual hours they had logged trying to keep things afloat.

From one angle, it looked like they were dropping the ball. From another angle, they were juggling three balls no one else realized existed.

As the picture widened, something interesting happened. The frustration softened. The accusations quieted. The tone changed.

It was not because the other department was perfect. Neither was it because mistakes hadn't been made. But because **everyone finally understood the angle.**

And once they saw the full picture, the conversation changed from:

"They're failing us," to **"How can we help lighten the load?"**

Perspective didn't erase the problem—it reframed it.

It turned blame into understanding, conflict into collaboration, and tension into teamwork.

That's the power of angle awareness.

When you shift from assuming the worst to understanding the angle, everything becomes easier to solve.

PERSPECTIVE ISN'T ABOUT AGREEMENT—IT'S ABOUT UNDERSTANDING

One of the biggest misunderstandings about perspective is the belief that if you *understand* someone, you must somehow be endorse, absorb, or agree with their viewpoint.

Not true.

You can understand someone without agreeing with them. You can respect someone without adopting their interpretation. You can acknowledge someone's angle without abandoning yours.

Understanding isn't surrender; it's clarity.

When you take the time to see the angle another person is standing in— the pressure they're under, the past they carry, the fears shaping their decisions—you gain insight, not obligation.

What that means is that you don't have to change your position to understand theirs. You don't have to soften your values to see where they're coming from. You don't have to erase your truth to recognize why their truth looks the way it does.

Perspective is not a compromise of identity. It's a strengthening of wisdom. When you understand someone's angle, their behavior makes sense—even if you still disagree with it.

Their intentions become clearer—even if their actions aren't justified.

Their choices become understandable—even if they're not choices you would make.

Perspective doesn't erase truth—it reveals it.

It shows the fuller picture. It brings hidden dynamics into view. It turns flat judgments into three-dimensional understanding.

You don't gain clarity by insisting the wall must look straight from only your angle. You gain clarity by walking around it—by seeing the lighting, the shadows, the distance, and the distortion. Only then can you understand what's really happening.

Perspective isn't about winning. It's about seeing.

And once you see clearly, you can respond wisely—without sacrificing your integrity, your boundaries, or your voice.

THE SHIFT FROM CONFUSION TO CONNECTION

Something powerful happens the moment you recognize how angles distort interpretation. Confusion begins to loosen its grip, and connection starts to take its place.

Once you understand how emotional lighting, distance, shadows, and angles shape what people *think* they see, you naturally begin to:

- **react with less intensity,** because not everything is a threat
- **respond with more patience,** because most reactions make sense once you know the angle
- **ask better questions,** because you're curious, not combative
- **give more grace,** because you realize you've misunderstood others too
- **assume less,** because assumptions thrive in narrow angles
- **notice more,** because clarity comes from paying attention to subtleties
- **speak with more accuracy,** because you're mindful of the interpretations your words land in
- **listen with more empathy,** because you understand that tone is shaped by story

Each of these shifts is subtle on its own—but together, they completely transform a conversation.

That is the power of understanding angles.

Once you see the angle someone is standing in, you stop fighting the person and start addressing the perspective.

You stop arguing about what happened and start exploring how it was experienced. You stop battling over the "crooked wall" and begin helping them see what you see—not by force, but by gently guiding them to a different vantage point.

It stops being: "You're wrong." It becomes: "Let's look at it from here."

The moment you shift your focus from winning the point to seeing the angle, connection becomes possible again.

And then, clarity follows.

Understanding angles doesn't just change how you communicate—it changes how you relate, how you interpret, and how you carry the weight of conflict. It moves you from confusion to connection, from reactivity to understanding, and from defending your truth to discovering a fuller truth with the other party.

THE SPACE BETWEEN PERSPECTIVES

How to Stay Connected When You Don't See the Same Way

Every conflict, every misunderstanding, every tense moment, every emotional reaction has one thing in common: a space between perspectives—a small but powerful gap where meanings diverge, assumptions multiply, and emotional reactions take shape.

Most people assume conflict happens when one person is wrong and the other is right. But more often, conflict happens when two people are both right from where *they're* standing. Their perspectives aren't wrong—they're simply different. And in that difference is the space where misunderstanding grows.

TWO GOOD MEN

On one of our projects, Jason and Brad were two of the most dependable guys on the crew. Both were skilled. Both were hardworking. Both respected each other. They weren't troublemakers, drama starters, or ego-driven personalities.

So when tension started showing up—short comments, stiff body language, quiet frustration—it caught my attention. These weren't guys who normally had issues. Something had shifted.

It began with something small.

Brad asked Jason to move a section of materials to clear a path for the next stage of the build. Jason said he would. But when Brad came back that afternoon, the materials were still untouched.

Brad felt irritated. Jason felt accused.

Brad saw it as a lack of follow-through, a slowdown that affected his next steps. Jason saw it as a simple misunderstanding of priorities since he had been finishing another task he believed was more urgent.

The next day, there was another small moment. Then another. Each one tiny on its own—barely worth mentioning. But small misunderstandings stack like hairline fractures in concrete: invisible at first, but eventually strong enough to split the slab.

I finally pulled them aside.

"What's going on between you two?" I asked.

They both sighed. They both shrugged. And then they both started talking—not over each other, not aggressively, but from two completely different emotional angles.

Brad said, "I just need Jason to do what he says he'll do. When something isn't done, it throws off my timeline."

Jason said, "I feel like Brad's constantly on me, like he doesn't trust my work or my judgment."

They were two good men with two honest perspectives and, more importantly, two completely different interpretations.

Neither of them was wrong. Neither of them was entirely right.

So what was happening?

They were standing in different worlds.

Brad was operating from **urgency**—deadlines, workflow, efficiency, the pressure of sequential tasks.

Jason was operating from **dignity**—craftsmanship, respect, pride in doing things well, not wanting to be micromanaged.

The details weren't the real conflict. **Their interpretations were.**

Once we slowed down and surfaced their angles, everything softened. Brad realized Jason wasn't ignoring him—Jason was prioritizing differently. Jason realized Brad wasn't attacking him—Brad was just trying to keep the build moving.

They were two good men who cared about the project. Two good men who cared about their work. Two good men who simply needed help seeing the angle the other was standing in.

And as soon as they did, the tension dissolved—not because anyone "won," but because clarity replaced assumption.

CONFLICT LIVES IN THE SPACE

Conflict doesn't live in the argument. It doesn't live in the words spoken, the tone used, or even the topic itself.

Conflict lives in the space between interpretations.

Two people stand in the same moment but see it through different emotional angles. That gap—that invisible space where meaning shifts and assumptions form—is where tension grows.

One person believes they're being clear; **the other feels confused.**

One believes they're being honest; **the other feels attacked.**

One believes they're helping; **the other feels controlled.**

One believes they're expressing concern; **the other feels criticized.**

From the outside, nothing dramatic is happening. But internally, both sides are having two very different experiences—and both feel true from where they stand.

That's the trouble with perspective:

The moment seems simple. The feelings around it are not.

Two people can hear the same sentence, be in the same room, have the same issue, and still walk away with completely different truths because each one filtered it through:

- their emotional angle
- their past experiences
- their insecurities
- their expectations
- their stress
- their assumptions

What happened matters far less than how each person interpreted what happened.

That's why arguments can feel disproportionate. It's why small misunderstandings become big fractures and conversations spiral even when everyone involved genuinely means well.

Conflict doesn't grow because people are bad at communicating. It grows because people are unaware of the *space* between their interpretations—and what's filling it.

Maybe it's fear.
Maybe it's history.
Maybe it's pressure.
Maybe it's insecurity.
Maybe it's exhaustion.
Maybe it's a story from childhood still echoing in the present.

Whatever fills that space determines whether the moment becomes connection or conflict.

The goal isn't to eliminate the space—that's impossible. The goal is to see it, understand it, and bridge it with curiosity instead of assumption.

The moment you recognize the space between interpretations, you stop fighting the other person and start exploring the space that exists between you.

And that's where conflict begins to dissolve, not because you agree but because you finally understand what each person was really seeing.

BRIDGING THE SPACE

Bridging the space between perspectives requires one skill that almost always gets forgotten in moments of tension:

Curiosity.

Not defensiveness. Not accusation. Not certainty. Not long explanations meant to defend your intentions.

Just curiosity.

Curiosity is the humility to admit, *"I might not be seeing everything."*

It's the courage to explore someone else's angle before insisting on your own. The openness that keeps a misunderstanding from becoming a battle.

Curiosity sounds like:

- **"What did you hear in what I said?"** (Because the meaning you sent may not be the meaning they received.)
- **"What part felt off to you?"** (Because the moment that triggered them might not be the one you think.)
- **"How did that come across from your angle?"** (Because their emotional position shaped their interpretation.)
- **"What were you assuming I meant?"** (Because assumptions fill the space faster than clarity does.)
- **"What did you need from me in that moment?"** (Because unmet needs often appear as irritation or withdrawal.)

Curiosity turns conflict into conversation, leads to the truth beneath the tension, and reveals the angle the other person is standing in. It forces you to stop reacting to the surface and start listening to the story behind it.

When curiosity enters a conversation:

- walls soften
- angles widen
- assumptions shrink
- tension releases
- empathy increases
- clarity expands
- connection rebuilds

Curiosity doesn't mean you agree. It doesn't mean you surrender your truth.

It simply means you care enough to explore their truth before defending yours. And when both people bring curiosity to a conflict, the space between them becomes something that can be bridged instead of something that divides.

Curiosity closes the gap. Every time.

THE THREE BRIDGES

When two people stand in different perspectives, there's always a gap between what one meant and what the other heard.

You can't eliminate that space—every relationship has it. What matters is how you bridge it.

There are **three bridges** that close the distance between interpretations. When used together, they turn conflict into connection instead of division.

1. Understanding

Not agreement—simply understanding.

Understanding means seeing why something made sense to the other person from *their* angle.

It sounds like:

- "I can see why you interpreted it that way."
- "From your perspective, that makes sense."
- "I get why that felt the way it did."

This doesn't mean you're admitting fault. It doesn't mean you're giving up your truth.

Understanding is the act of stepping into someone else's vantage point long enough to see what the moment looked like through their eyes.

It neutralizes defensiveness almost instantly because people calm down when they feel seen.

2. Acknowledgment

Recognizing the emotional reality beneath the reaction.

Acknowledgment validates the feeling behind the interpretation, even if the interpretation itself wasn't accurate.

It sounds like:

- "I get why that frustrated you."
- "I understand why that stung."
- "I hear that this felt dismissive to you."

You're not confirming that their perspective was *correct*. You're confirming that their emotion was real.

This bridge tells the other person, "Your experience matters, even if we saw it differently."

That alone can dissolve 80% of tension.

3. Adjustment

A small shift now prevents a big misunderstanding later.

Adjustment is where connection becomes practical. It's the small communication tweak that keeps future conversations cleaner, clearer, and less emotionally loaded.

It sounds like:

- "Next time, I'll give more context."
- "I'll check in before assuming."
- "I'll slow down so it doesn't come across harsh."

You're not saying, "I was wrong." What you're saying is, "I'm willing to grow."

Adjustment has enormous impact because it restores safety. It proves the relationship matters more than the moment.

THE POWER OF ALL THREE

Any one of these bridges helps. Two of them help more.

However, when **all three** are practiced together, something powerful happens:

- misunderstandings shrink
- trust deepens
- egos soften
- defenses lower
- connection strengthens

This way, relationships don't weaken after conflict.

They get stronger.

Because the goal isn't to avoid the space between perspectives—it's to build bridges across it.

The more often you use these three bridges, the shorter that space becomes, until understanding feels almost automatic and conflict becomes far less threatening.

THE SUBTLE ART OF STAYING IN THE CONVERSATION

Most people don't struggle because they communicate poorly. They struggle because they **leave conversations too early.**

Not physically at first. They leave emotionally.

The moment discomfort rises, most people retreat. They shut down, become quiet, get sharp, or change the subject. They walk away mentally long before they walk away physically. Why? Because discomfort tricks the mind into believing that leaving will reduce the tension.

But it doesn't.

When you exit the conversation too soon—whether through silence, sarcasm, withdrawal, or defensiveness—**the space between perspectives widens.**

Misunderstanding deepens and assumptions take root. The conflict becomes harder to repair, not easier.

Staying in the conversation does **not** mean tolerating disrespect. Neither does it mean agreeing or abandoning your boundaries.

Staying in the conversation simply means remaining open, present, and engaged long enough for clarity to surface. Because clarity rarely appears in the first two minutes of tension. It emerges in the space you create when you choose to stay.

Here are **five practical ways** to stay in difficult conversations without losing yourself:

1. Slow the pace.

Fast talking is fast reacting. It turns the moment into emotional sparring—one misunderstanding thrown at another.

When you slow down your speech, your breathing, and your tone, you shift the conversation from:

- reaction → understanding
- speed → clarity
- threat → collaboration

Slow talking becomes problem-solving. It gives both people enough emotional room to think, not just defend.

2. Remove assumption words.

Some words ignite defensiveness instantly:

- "You always…"
- "You never…"
- "You don't care…"
- "You're just being…"

These words don't describe reality. They describe emotional exaggeration—the mind trying to express hurt by using absolutes. Assumption words turn a momentary issue into a character attack, which guarantees escalation.

Removing them keeps the conversation focused on the situation, not the person.

3. Notice emotional shifts.

Before someone shuts down, there are small signals:

- a sudden pause
- a shoulder drop
- crossed arms
- a sigh
- pacing
- breaking eye contact
- a step back

These shifts aren't irritations to ignore. They're warning indicators saying, "The space between us is widening. Slow down."

Noticing these cues is one of the most powerful skills in communication. It lets you adjust before the conversation fractures.

4. Ask clarifying questions.

Clarifying questions re-open the door that defensiveness tries to close.

Questions like:

- "What did you hear when I said that?"
- "What part felt true or untrue to you?"
- "What were you trying to communicate in that moment?"
- "Help me understand what mattered most to you here."

These questions shift the conversation from accusation to exploration, from certainty to curiosity, and from assumption to understanding.

They bring hidden angles into the light.

5. Give reassurance where needed.

Sometimes people can't hear logic until they feel safe. Their nervous system won't accept information while it's bracing for rejection, attack, or blame.

A simple reassurance like:

- "I'm not attacking you."
- "I care about us."
- "I'm not going anywhere."
- "I just want to understand."

can calm the emotional current enough to keep the conversation alive.

Reassurance is not weakness; it's strategic clarity.

WHY STAYING MATTERS

People don't need perfect communication. They need **presence**—someone who will stay long enough to understand what's actually happening rather than what the moment makes them assume.

Staying in the conversation doesn't guarantee agreement. But it does guarantee connection—or, at the very least, the opportunity for clarity.

Because most conflicts don't break relationships.

Avoiding the conversations that could resolve them does.

A MARRIAGE EXAMPLE

A friend once explained something to me that completely changed the way I listen in relationships.

He said, "When my wife says, 'We never spend time together,' she doesn't actually mean *never*. She means she feels distant… and doesn't know how to put that feeling into words yet."

Her **phrasing** wasn't accurate. But her **emotion** was.

There was a space—a gap—between what she said and what she meant. And in that gap, he had a choice:

He could react to the **words**, or he could respond to the **feeling**.

When he reacted to the words, it always went wrong:

- "That's not true."
- "We just went out last weekend."
- "I've been here every night this week."

He was fact-checking her sentence. The issue, however, was that she wasn't asking for accuracy—she was asking for closeness.

Consequently, every logical rebuttal pushed them farther apart. The space widened. She felt unheard, and he felt misunderstood. But when he learned to respond to the feeling underneath the phrase, everything changed.

Instead of arguing the wording, he began saying things like:

- "You're feeling disconnected, huh?"

- "It sounds like you miss us."
- "You want more time that feels like *us*, not just being in the same room."

The shift was instant.

Her defensiveness softened. His frustration disappeared. The emotional angle he had missed suddenly came into view.

The space closed—not because he agreed with the literal words, but because he understood the emotional message.

This is the heart of perspective in relationships:

Most people don't tell you exactly what they feel. They tell you the closest sentence their emotion can reach.

Your job isn't to argue the accuracy of the sentence. Your job is to hear the emotion the person couldn't quite articulate. Because in marriage—and in every close relationship—responding to the feeling is almost always more powerful than reacting to the words.

THE SPACE IS WHERE HEALING HAPPENS

Healing doesn't happen when two people finally agree. It doesn't even require two people to see the situation the same way.

Healing happens when two people are willing to stand in the space between their perspectives long enough to understand each other.

Most relationships break not because the perspectives are too far apart, but because no one is willing to stay in the space between them.

The space is uncomfortable. It's uncertain. It's vulnerable. It's the place where your truth meets their truth—the place where you're both confronted with angles, emotions, and interpretations you didn't expect.

But that's also the place where real connection begins.

As mentioned earlier, you don't eliminate the space. You learn to navigate and breathe in it. You learn to stay steady in it.

You learn to say things like:

- **"I see your angle."** Not "you're right," but "I see what you were seeing."
- **"I understand your experience."** Not "I felt the same way," but "your feelings make sense."
- **"I respect your perspective."** Not "I'm abandoning my viewpoint," but "your viewpoint matters too."

These sentences build a bridge in the space where misunderstanding normally grows. They soften what was tense, steady what felt unstable, and calm what was spiraling.

Connection isn't built through perfect communication. Connection is built when two people are willing to stand in the same uncomfortable space
and *not* run away.

The space is where:

- assumptions are clarified
- fears are named
- intentions are understood
- emotions are validated
- stories are revealed
- trust begins again

Healing happens when you stay long enough in that space to see not just the moment, but the person standing inside it. You don't need to merge perspectives to heal. You simply need the courage to meet each other in the space between them.

That space is where understanding grows. It's where trust rebuilds and relationships deepen.

The space is not the problem. The space is where healing happens.

SIDE QUEST 1: "Walk Around the Wall"

Tagline: See it from their angle—literally.

Description:

The reader physically practices stepping into another perspective.

Action Steps:

1. Choose one recurring point of tension with someone in your life.
2. Take a blank sheet of paper. Draw two stick figures in two of the corners.
3. Write *your* interpretation under one figure.
4. Write *their possible interpretation* under the other—without assuming negativity.
5. Ask the bridge question: **"What might this look like from their side?"**
6. Rewrite the moment from their emotional lens, not your own.

Outcome: An "aha" moment by physically seeing perspective contrast.

SIDE QUEST 2: "The Listening Level Challenge"

Tagline: Master silence. Upgrade connection.

Action Steps:

For one day:

1. Don't interrupt.
2. Reflect back before responding.
3. Ask one clarifying question.
4. Notice emotional cues (shoulders drop, tone softens).

Outcome: A measurable increase in empathy and clarity in conversations.

SIDE QUEST 3: "The Language Swap"

Tagline: Change your words, change the moment.

Action Steps:

1. For the next 3 conversations, replace reactive statements with curiosity-based ones.
2. Use these replacements:

   - "Why would you do that?" → "Help me understand that choice."

   - "That's not what I meant." → "Tell me what you heard."

   - "You're overreacting." → "What part felt the hardest?"

Outcome: A first-hand experience of how communication shifts when clarity replaces defensiveness.

PART II
UNDERSTANDING YOURSELF

THE LANGUAGE OF TRUST

Rebuilding Connection When the Frame Has Shifted

Every relationship—personal, professional, romantic, or family—runs on one thing:

Trust.

Not communication. Not compatibility. Not shared interests.

Without trust, communication becomes guarded and connection becomes thin. Without trust, every interaction feels heavier than it needs to be.

Trust isn't something you *have* or *don't have*. It's something you build—or break—moment by moment, interaction by interaction.

THE CRACKED BEAM

When I was younger I ran a framing crew for my dad.

One day we were framing a home when one of the guys called me over.

"Dustin, this beam doesn't look right," he informed.

I walked over and saw it—a subtle crack running through a key structural beam. Not enough to cause a collapse. Not enough to alarm the untrained eye. Not even enough to be obvious.

But enough to weaken the structure if we ignored it.

From a distance, the beam looked fine. If you weren't looking closely, you'd never catch the issue. It would've been easy to call it "good enough" and move on.

But a crack in a load-bearing beam is never "just a crack." It's a risk multiplier. A weakness that grows under pressure. A vulnerability that hides behind layers of drywall and paint.

So we replaced the beam. We reinforced the frame and made sure the structure was solid before anything else was built on top of it.

And as I watched the crew work, the metaphor hit me:

Trust is a structural beam. And small cracks weaken everything built on top of it.

TRUST ISN'T LOST IN BIG MOMENTS — IT'S LOST IN SMALL ONES

People almost never lose trust over one catastrophic failure. Trust rarely breaks in a single dramatic moment.

It erodes slowly through:

- a promise forgotten
- a tone that feels dismissive
- a lack of follow-through
- a missing detail
- a defensive reaction
- an assumption made
- a feeling ignored
- a concern downplayed
- a need overlooked

Little cracks. Small fractures. Hidden vulnerabilities.

A single crack won't break a relationship. **But leaving it unaddressed will.**

TWO TYPES OF TRUST

Trust isn't one thing—it's two interconnected forms.

1. Trust of Integrity

This is the moral foundation

"Do you mean what you say?"

"Can I rely on your word?"
"Are you honest, ethical, and consistent?"

Integrity trust answers the question: **"Can I trust your character?"**

2. Trust of Awareness

This is the emotional foundation.

"Do you understand me?"
"Are you aware of how your actions affect me?"
"Do you see what I need?"
"Do you notice my emotional world?"

Awareness trust answers the question: **"Can I trust your consideration?"**

You can have one without the other.

Someone can be:

- honest, but unaware
- ethical, but emotionally disconnected
- responsible, but relationally careless
- reliable, but dismissive
- consistent in action, but inconsistent in empathy

Healthy trust requires both integrity and awareness.

WHY AWARENESS MATTERS MORE THAN PEOPLE THINK

Years ago, a client called frustrated about a project delay.

I explained everything logically. Step by step. Detail by detail.

Every reason was legitimate, but she still felt upset. At first, I couldn't understand it—the logic was airtight.

Then it clicked: I was speaking to her *logic*. She needed me to speak to her *stress*.

She didn't need facts; she needed reassurance. She didn't need timelines; she needed acknowledgment. She didn't need an explanation; she needed **awareness**.

Once I paused and said, "I get why this stressed you out—this project means a lot to you.
 We're going to make it right," everything changed.

Logic earns respect. Awareness earns trust.

THE FIVE PILLARS OF TRUST REPAIR

When trust cracks, here's the way I have found best to repair it:

1. Acknowledgment

Not excuses, justification, or technical explanations.

Just acknowledgment.

"I see what I did."

"I understand how that affected you."

2. Ownership

Responsibility without defense.

"That was on me."

"I should've handled that differently."

3. Clarity

Explain what you'll do differently—not to defend the past, but to shape the future.

"Next time, I'll communicate sooner."

"From now on, I'll check in first."

4. Consistency

Trust is rebuilt through repeated aligned actions.

Show it. Don't just say it.

5. Patience

You can't rush someone's healing. Consistency over time rebuilds the trust your words opened the door to.

A LEADERSHIP STORY ABOUT TRUST

Years ago, when I was living in Kansas City, a team member came to me frustrated. Not angry, just discouraged.

He said, "I don't think my input matters."

We talked, and I realized something important:

He didn't need a new system. Neither did he need a new meeting format or a big leadership overhaul.

He needed emotional visibility—to be seen, valued, and included.

So I became intentional. I started calling him by name, asking for his perspective, thanking him for his input, and highlighting his contributions in front of others.

His posture changed almost immediately. His engagement returned and his confidence grew. Nothing was wrong with his competence. He was starving for awareness.

TRUST MAKES COMMUNICATION EFFORTLESS

When trust is strong:

- you can say less and mean more
- you can speak plainly without fear
- you can address conflict without defensiveness
- you can share concerns without tension
- misunderstandings resolve quickly
- assumptions fade

In contrast, when trust is weak:

- simple questions feel like criticism
- neutral comments feel like disrespect
- honest feedback feels like an attack
- requests feel like demands
- everything becomes emotionally amplified

With trust, communication becomes connection.

Without trust, communication becomes interpretation.

THE LANGUAGE OF TRUST

Certain phrases strengthen trust immediately:

- "I can see why you felt that way."
- "Thanks for telling me."
- "I should've communicated that better."
- "I'm listening."
- "What do you need from me right now?"
- "I want us to understand each other."
- "I'm not going anywhere."

And certain phrases fracture trust just as quickly:

- "You're overreacting."
- "Stop twisting what I said."
- "You're being dramatic."
- "You always think the worst."
- "Why are you making this a big deal?"

Trust isn't built through perfection. It's built through **presence.**

Being someone who listens. Someone who notices. Someone who cares. Someone who owns their part. Someone who adjusts. Someone who shows up consistently.

Trust is built slowly and lost quickly. But when you understand how trust works—you can strengthen every relationship you have.

PERSPECTIVE PRACTICE

Living with Awareness, Curiosity, and Connection

Perspective isn't a moment of inspiration—it's a discipline.

It's something you train, sharpen, and return to again and again until it becomes part of how you see the world. Most people assume perspective is a personality trait, that some people are naturally good at understanding others, and some aren't.

But that's simply not true.

Perspective is a muscle.

And like any muscle, it becomes stronger with use and weaker with neglect.

THE TRAIL CLIMB

There's a trail in Southern Utah that overlooks the red rock canyons— ridges that drop into sweeping views of sandstone cliffs and wide-open sky. I've walked it dozens of times, but the first time I hiked it, I remember stopping near the top where the trail narrows and the landscape opens like a curtain.

From the bottom, the climb looks rugged and chaotic. From halfway up, the view improves, but it's still obstructed. But from the top, everything makes sense.

What looked like chaos becomes harmony. What looked like a steep scramble becomes a clear path. What felt overwhelming becomes beautiful.

It wasn't the trail that changed—**it was the vantage point.**

Life works the same way.

Sometimes you're standing too close to something to see it clearly. Sometimes your emotional angle distorts the truth.

Sometimes you need elevation—not escape—to finally understand.

PERSPECTIVE REQUIRES ELEVATION

When you emotionally zoom out, you start seeing:

- the pattern you keep repeating
- the fear behind someone's reaction
- the insecurity behind someone's tone
- the weight behind someone's silence
- the truth beneath your own frustration

But it's hard to see any of this when you're still in the moment.

Perspective isn't granted—it's chosen. It requires deliberate pause. It requires intentional distance.

And sometimes, even a three-second pause can change your entire interpretation.

WHY PEOPLE LOSE PERSPECTIVE

People don't lose perspective because they're weak. They lose perspective because they're overwhelmed—by stress, deadlines, expectations, fear of failure, emotional fatigue, relational history, and old wounds resurfacing in the present.

When emotions get loud, perspective becomes quiet.

Think about it:

- When you're stressed, everything feels urgent.
- When you're tired, everything feels heavier.
- When you're afraid, everything feels threatening.
- When you're insecure, everything feels personal.
- When you're hurt, everything feels intentional.

Perspective dissolves under emotional pressure—**unless you practice holding onto it.**

THE THREE PRACTICES OF PERSPECTIVE

There are three core practices that build everyday perspective.

They're simple—but not easy. And they will absolutely change the way you see and respond to the world if you integrate them consistently.

1. The Practice of Pause

Before reacting, pause. Before assuming, pause. Before responding, pause.

The pause is not weakness—it's wisdom.

It prevents you from reacting to your first interpretation and expands your mind before your emotion contracts it. It gives your heart time to settle so your clarity can rise.

A two-second pause can save a relationship.
A five-second pause can prevent an argument.
A ten-second pause can change how safe someone feels with you forever.

Practice the pause until it becomes instinct.

2. The Practice of Curiosity

Curiosity dissolves defensiveness. It moves conversations from *collision* to *connection*.

When something feels off, ask:

- "What else could be true?"
- "What might they be feeling?"
- "What did they hear in what I said?"
- "What angle are they seeing this from?"
- "What disappointment or pressure is shaping their reaction?"

Curiosity shifts your posture:

- from judgment → exploration
- from accusation → understanding
- from frustration → discovery

Curiosity widens your emotional range.

Again, it doesn't mean you agree—**it means you're open.**

3. The Practice of Compassion

Compassion recognizes that everyone is carrying an unseen load.

People miscommunicate because they're tired.
People snap because they're overwhelmed.
People shut down because they're scared.
People avoid because they're ashamed.
People overreact because something old got triggered inside something new.

Compassion isn't softness—it's strength. It allows you to hold your boundaries while still holding space for someone else's humanity.

Compassion doesn't excuse poor behavior. It explains why it happened and helps you address the wound beneath it.

Compassion is **perspective in action.**

YOUR PERSPECTIVE WILL DROP — EXPECT IT

No one maintains perfect perspective all the time.

You will get tired. You will get emotional. You will get overwhelmed. You will lose sight of the deeper truth.

That's normal.

What matters is **how quickly you return.**

If you lose perspective and regain it in an hour—that's growth.
If it takes a day—that's progress.
If it takes a week—that's resilience.

The goal isn't perfection; it's recovery.

Perspective is the ability to return to clarity faster each time.

A MOMENT WHEN I LOST PERSPECTIVE

I remember a day when everything piled up at once.

Deadlines. Subcontractors running behind. Weather delays. A client upset about a small detail. Family needing my attention. My own expectations stacking on my shoulders.

That day, I snapped at someone who didn't deserve it. My tone was short. My patience was thin. My clarity was nowhere to be found.

Later, sitting in my truck with the engine idling, I could finally see it:

It wasn't about them. It was about me—my exhaustion, my stress, my internal load.

Perspective returned, and with it, humility. I apologized. We reset. The relationship strengthened.

Not because I handled everything perfectly—but because I practiced returning to clarity.

THE DAILY PRACTICES OF PERSPECTIVE

Perspective doesn't grow by accident.

It grows through intentional daily habits:

- **Morning grounding**—pause before the day pulls you in.
- **Name your emotional state**—"I'm stressed," "I'm overwhelmed," "I'm tired."
- **Ask one perspective question daily**—"What am I not seeing?"
- **Nightly reflection**—"Where did I lose perspective today?"
- **Give people the benefit of the doubt**—grace is perspective in disguise.
- **Step away for clarity, not escape**—distance creates vision.
- **Choose curiosity over certainty**—always.

Perspective isn't an event. **It's a lifestyle.**

And the more you practice it, the more your relationships, communication, reactions, and leadership transform in powerful and lasting ways.

THE BLUEPRINT OF PERCEPTION

Understanding the Five Builders of Perspective

Every person sees the world through a blueprint—a hidden internal plan shaped by upbringing, culture, experience, emotion, and identity. This internal blueprint determines how we interpret moments, conversations, tone, silence, intentions, and people.

Most people never realize they're carrying one. They assume they see the world "as it is." But the truth is, no one sees the world as it is.

We all see the world as we are.

Two people can hear the same sentence and leave with completely different meanings because their blueprints were drafted from entirely different histories.

Understanding someone's blueprint doesn't just improve communication—**it changes how you interpret human behavior as a whole.**

THE FIVE BUILDERS

Just as a home's blueprint is shaped by an architect's choices, your perception is shaped by five internal builders that constructed your worldview long before you had the slightest idea. If you've ever wondered why two people interpret the same moment differently, these builders hold the answer.

Let's walk through each one.

1. Upbringing

Your family is your first architect.

Before you can speak, your environment is already teaching you how to see the world.

The way caregivers spoke to you, corrected you, encouraged you, disciplined you, or dismissed you shaped your blueprint long before you understood what a blueprint was.

- If you grew up in a home where emotions were minimized, you learned to suppress feelings—in yourself and in others.
- If conflict was constant, intensity became a warning sign.
- If affection was limited, closeness became unfamiliar territory.
- If love was secure, you learned to interpret kindness as normal, not suspicious.
- If approval was inconsistent, you learned to chase it.

You didn't choose your original blueprint—**you inherited it.**

But the good thing is that you have the absolute ability to rebuild it.

2. Culture

Culture shapes what you consider normal, polite, respectful, rude, acceptable, or taboo.

Your culture teaches you:

- how to speak
- how to disagree
- how to apologize
- how to express emotion
- how to show respect
- how to interpret authority
- how to enter or exit social situations
- how to define loyalty, love, and boundaries

What feels offensive in one culture feels honest in another. In the same vein, what feels rude in one environment feels confident in another.

Culture is the **silent architect of assumptions**—and assumptions are the fuel of misunderstanding.

3. Experience

Your personal history forms expectations—often without your permission.

This builder teaches your brain patterns:

- A person who's been betrayed interprets uncertainty as threat.
- A person who's been supported interprets uncertainty as possibility.
- A person who's been criticized interprets feedback as rejection.
- A person who's been encouraged interprets feedback as growth.

Your brain is fast—faster than your awareness. It interprets meaning based on old data before you consciously think.

Experience creates **emotional reflexes**:

- You flinch emotionally when something resembles past pain.
- You brace for impact when someone raises their voice.
- You shrink or over-explain when criticism sounds familiar.
- You assume rejection before it appears.

Your reactions are not random—they're echoes of your experiences.

4. Emotion

Emotion is the most immediate builder—the one active right now.

You don't initially interpret situations logically. You interpret them emotionally first.

Emotion colors perception instantly:

- When you're peaceful, the world feels open.
- When you're anxious, the world feels threatening.
- When you're tired, everything feels heavier.
- When you're hopeful, everything feels possible.
- When you're hurt, everything feels personal.

Emotions don't distort reality—**they flavor it.**

And just like seasoning, the flavor determines how the whole moment tastes, even when the ingredients are the same.

5. Identity

Identity is the deepest builder—the bedrock beneath the others.

Identity shapes:

- what you believe you deserve
- what you believe you can handle
- what you believe others think of you
- what you believe love should look like
- what you believe people intend
- what you believe your role is in relationships

Identity determines what feels true before you think it through.

- A person who believes they're unworthy interprets kindness with suspicion.
- A person who believes they're strong interprets obstacles as temporary.
- A person who believes they're a burden interprets requests as guilt.
- A person who believes they are valuable interprets challenge as opportunity.

Identity is the **hidden foundation** beneath every reaction.

REWRITING YOUR BLUEPRINT

Here's the most empowering truth in this chapter:

You can rebuild your blueprint.

Your upbringing started it.
Culture shaped it.
Experience reinforced it.
Emotion colors it.
Identity anchors it.

But the blueprint you inherited is not the blueprint you're required to live by.

You can redraw the lines. You can challenge old interpretations. You can replace outdated emotional reflexes and choose healthier beliefs, boundaries, and meanings.

Rewriting your blueprint begins with awareness:

- "That reaction wasn't about them—it was my blueprint."
- "That irritation was old, not new."
- "That insecurity came from my past, not this moment."
- "That assumption came from fear, not fact."

Awareness breaks automatic interpretation and gives you the pen. It allows you to build a new internal plan.

BLUEPRINT EXERCISES

These exercises help you learn your blueprint and start rewriting it.

1. Identify your primary builder.

Which builder is shaping your reactions most right now? Is it upbringing? Culture? Emotion? Experience? Identity?

2. Notice emotional reflexes.

When you react quickly, pause and ask, **"Is this response old or new?"**

3. Rewrite one belief per week.

Challenge an outdated narrative.

For example: "People aren't disappointed in me—I'm projecting an old story."

4. Anchor new identity statements.

Repeat them until your mind believes them:

- "I am worth listening to."
- "I can handle conflict with clarity."
- "I don't have to predict others' intentions."
- "I am allowed to take up space."

Blueprints don't change overnight. They change over time—through awareness, repetition, and honest reflection.

WHY THE BLUEPRINT MATTERS

When you understand your blueprint, you stop reacting unconsciously.

You start:

- speaking more gently
- listening more intentionally
- assuming less
- noticing more
- extending grace
- expressing needs clearly
- separating past pain from present moments

When you understand someone else's blueprint, you stop taking things personally.

You begin to:

- acknowledge their fear
- honor their experience
- understand their tone
- respect their emotional angle
- lead with empathy

The blueprint of perception is one of the most transformative tools in communication.

Because once you understand the blueprint, you finally understand the person—**even if that person is you.**

THE RELATIONSHIP BLUEPRINT

Building Connection Through Contrast

Every relationship has a blueprint—spoken or unspoken, clear or vague, conscious or unconscious. A relational blueprint isn't just a plan; it's the shared understanding of **how things work between two people**. It's how you speak, how you connect, how you repair, how you show love, and how you handle tension.

When the blueprint is aligned, relationships feel natural. However, when the blueprint is mismatched, everything feels heavier than it should.

Most couples, families, friends, and teams never talk about their relational blueprint. They assume the other person builds relationships the same way they do. And when they don't, frustration grows quietly in the background like slow water eroding stone.

You can love someone deeply and still misunderstand them completely. You can be committed to someone and still misinterpret their intentions.

Love doesn't guarantee alignment; understanding does.

THE KITCHEN CONVERSATION

A couple I know once shared a story that stayed with me.

Late one night, they were standing in their kitchen after a long argument neither of them wanted to have. The shouting had stopped; the emotional exhaustion hadn't. They were drained—not from malice, but from trying for two hours to understand each other and failing. They weren't fighting about chores or schedules or money.

They were fighting about **meaning.**

He felt unappreciated; she felt unheard. He felt misunderstood; she felt alone in her effort.

Finally, she leaned against the counter, tears gathering, and said quietly, **"I just need you to help me feel safe."**

He looked at her, confused. "Safe? What do you mean safe? I would never hurt you."

She shook her head.

"Not physical safety…emotional safety," she clarified, her tone frustrated but soft. "Safety to tell you how I feel without it turning into a fight."

Right there—in the quiet, vulnerable space of that kitchen—their blueprints were laid bare.

That was the blueprint she needed. And it wasn't the one he had been building.

He believed that being strong, solving problems, fixing issues, and providing stability created safety. She needed softness, presence, gentleness and emotional room to breathe.

Same relationship. Two different blueprints.

And neither realized it until that moment.

BLUEPRINTS AREN'T RIGHT OR WRONG —THEY'RE LEARNED

Everyone learns relational patterns from somewhere:

- How your parents argued—or avoided arguing.
- How affection was given—or withheld.
- How boundaries were honored—or ignored.
- How needs were expressed—or silenced.
- How apologies were modeled—or never modeled.
- How emotional availability was shown—or absent.

Your relationship blueprint is built long before your adult relationships begin.

And that blueprint influences:

- how you show love
- how you interpret love
- how you express emotion
- how you handle disappointment
- how you deal with conflict
- how you communicate needs
- how willing you are to be vulnerable
- how safe you feel opening up

You're not reacting to people as they are—you're reacting to people through the blueprint you learned.

THE THREE BLUEPRINT LANGUAGES

Most people operate primarily through one dominant relational language. And conflict almost always comes from speaking different ones.

1. Emotional Blueprint

People with an emotional blueprint build relationships around connection, affection, tone, closeness, and the emotional "temperature" of the room. They read *how* things feel more than *what* is happening.

Key needs:

- warmth
- reassurance
- presence
- gentleness
- emotional safety

When these needs aren't met, they often feel insecure, distant, or disconnected—even when the relationship looks fine on paper.

2. Functional Blueprint

These people build relationships through action, responsibility, service, and reliability. They show love by *doing*—not by talking.

Key needs:

- stability
- follow-through
- shared responsibilities
- clear expectations
- competent partnership

When these needs aren't met, they feel overwhelmed, unappreciated, or taken for granted.

3. Vision Blueprint

These people build relationships around shared purpose, big-picture goals, dreams, and unity of direction. They feel connected through future alignment.

Key needs:

- unity
- partnership
- direction
- shared values
- mutual growth

When these needs aren't met, they feel stuck, unseen, or disconnected from purpose.

CONFLICT HAPPENS WHEN BLUEPRINTS COLLIDE

Consider this example:

A husband with a **functional blueprint** comes home exhausted and starts doing dishes to show he cares. His wife, who has an **emotional blueprint** interprets his silence as distance.

He thinks, 'I'm helping. I'm showing love.'

She thinks, 'He's upset. Something's wrong. He's pulling away.'

Same moment. Different blueprints. Growing distance.

Or this:

A wife with an emotional blueprint shares her frustrations from the day. Her husband with a functional blueprint offers solutions—not empathy.

She feels unheard. He feels confused. Both feel frustrated.

Not because they're incompatible—but because they're speaking different blueprint languages.

YOU DON'T NEED THE SAME BLUEPRINT — YOU NEED A SHARED ONE

People don't need identical relational styles to have an extraordinary connection. They simply need to understand each other's blueprints and create a shared one.

A shared blueprint is a fusion of what works for both parties in a relationship. It doesn't imply erasing either party's blueprint language or forcing them to 'conform.' As the name implies, a shared blueprint brings the core elements of both parties' blueprints together, making them a team and not competitors.

A shared blueprint answers questions like:

- How do we handle conflict?
- How do we communicate needs?
- How do we express appreciation?
- How do we repair quickly?
- What does emotional safety look like for us?
- What does support look like for each person?

When these things are clear, connection flows naturally.

THE PERSPECTIVE TRIAD IN RELATIONSHIPS

To build a shared blueprint, you need three pillars:

1. Understanding

Know the emotional world the other person lives in.

2. Respect

Honor their blueprint—even when it's different from yours.

3. Adjustment

This is where intentional work comes in.

Shift your approach to meet them where they are.

When all three are active, relationships don't just survive—they transform.

THE BLUEPRINT EXERCISE FOR COUPLES & FAMILIES

Ask each other:

- "What do you need to feel safe with me?"
- "What makes you feel appreciated?"
- "What makes you shut down?"
- "What do you wish I understood about you?"
- "What does emotional connection look like to you?"

People reveal their blueprint through their answers—often without even realizing it.

MISALIGNMENT DOESN'T MEAN MISMATCH

Most relationships aren't struggling because the people are incompatible. They're struggling because the blueprints have never been compared, aligned, or updated.

And here's the hope:

You can rebuild a blueprint at any time.

You're not stuck with the model you inherited. You're free to build a new one together.

Relationships don't need perfect communication.

They need shared understanding.

C H A P T E R   1 0

THE LEADERSHIP LENS

Leading People Who See the World Differently

Leadership isn't about authority—**it's about perspective.**

The best leaders aren't the ones who talk the most, know the most, or demand the most. They're the ones who **see the most.**

They see people clearly. They see problems accurately. They see potential instinctively. They see solutions others overlook. And most importantly—they see the unseen emotional currents guiding behavior.

A leader with perspective leads with wisdom, calm, and clarity. A leader without perspective, on the other hand, leads with pressure, frustration, and reaction.

Leadership is not simply influence. **Leadership is emotional vision.**

LEADERSHIP IS EMOTIONAL VISION

Too many leaders rely on skill but neglect perspective.

Skill builds projects while **perspective builds people**—and people build everything else.

A leader with perspective can repair trust without creating drama. A leader without perspective can break trust without realizing it.

Perspective is the difference between reacting to behavior and understanding the story behind it.

TEAM MEETING

I once walked into a meeting where two teams—both talented, both hardworking—were clashing. Their tasks overlapped, their timelines tangled, and every small delay was magnified by stress.

When I stepped into the room, I didn't start with a timeline, a task list, or a call out of what went wrong. I looked around the table and saw:

- one guy leaning forward, tense
- another leaning back, guarded
- someone with arms crossed, frustrated
- someone sighing every few seconds
- someone staring at the floor, overwhelmed

I realized instantly that it wasn't a scheduling or communication problem. It wasn't even a workload problem.

It was an emotional problem.

Stress. Pressure. Fear. Misinterpretation. Insecurity. Frustration.

Those were the real drivers of the tension.

So instead of asking, "What happened?" I suggested, **"Let's talk about what each team is carrying right now."**

Not tasks. Not deadlines or complaints.

Load.

One team explained the pressure they were under. The other explained the obstacles they were facing. As they listened, the tension dissolved—not because the work changed, but because **their perspective changed.**

Once people understood each other's load, they stopped blaming each other for it.

THREE C'S OF LEADERSHIP PERSPECTIVE

Every great leader practices three core perspective skills. They look simple, but they're transformative when done right.

1. Clarity

Clarity keeps teams aligned. It reduces anxiety and builds trust. Clarity is not giving *more* information—it's giving the **right** information.

Clarity answers:

- What matters most?
- What comes first?
- What does "done" look like?
- What's the win?
- Who owns what?

With clarity, teams accelerate. But without it, teams drift.

2. Compassion

Compassion understands that people aren't machines—they are emotional beings with fears, limits, stories, and pressures.

Compassion sees:

- the stress beneath the silence
- the fear beneath the frustration
- the insecurity beneath the defensiveness
- the pressure beneath the mistakes

Compassion does **not** lower standards. Compassion raises understanding—and understanding raises performance.

3. Communication

Communication is the bridge between clarity and compassion. It carries vision, values, expectations, and encouragement.

Great leaders talk **with** people; poor leaders talk **at** people.

Great leaders inspire effort; poor leaders demand effort.

Great leaders lean on trust; poor leaders lean on authority.

Communication isn't about volume.

It's about connection.

PSYCHOLOGICAL SAFETY: THE SECRET INGREDIENT

Teams perform at their highest when they feel safe to:

- ask questions
- admit mistakes
- express concerns
- offer feedback
- challenge ideas respectfully

Psychological safety doesn't make teams soft. It makes them unstoppable.

People do their best work when they aren't bracing for criticism, judgment, or embarrassment. When people feel safe, they bring more ideas, more energy, more ownership, and more honesty. When they don't feel safe, they play small—even if they're incredibly capable.

LEADERSHIP ADJUSTMENT

Years ago in Kansas City, one of my team leads was struggling.

It wasn't because he lacked skill—he was excellent technically—but because he lacked perspective.

He communicated through pressure, believed intensity equaled leadership, interpreted silence as defiance, and read questions as challenges to his authority.

His team began shutting down. Morale, engagement, productivity—all dropped.

I pulled him aside and told him, **"Strength isn't volume. Leadership isn't pressure—it's clarity."**

We talked through his blueprint—how he grew up with the belief that leadership meant force, that emotion meant weakness, and that questions meant disrespect.

Once he saw his perspective, he could shift it.

Within weeks, everything changed. He didn't become "softer." He became clearer. Calmer. More aware.

And because he changed his perspective, his team had a changed experience of his leadership.

PERSPECTIVE MAKES LEADERS MAGNETIC

People follow leaders who:

- see them
- understand them
- challenge them
- believe in them
- speak to their potential
- treat them with dignity
- build trust consistently

These leaders don't need to demand loyalty. They earn it—naturally.

People don't follow titles; they follow perspective.

LEADERSHIP WITHOUT PERSPECTIVE IS BLIND

When a leader has no perspective:

- every disagreement feels like defiance
- every question feels like disrespect
- every mistake feels like incompetence
- every delay feels like laziness
- every emotion feels like drama

However, with perspective:

- disagreements become data
- questions become clarity tools
- mistakes become teaching moments
- delays become problem-solving opportunities
- emotions become insight

Perspective doesn't just make you a better leader—it makes the leadership load lighter.

How?

When you change the way you see people, there is a palpable change in how they experience your leadership.

WHEN PEOPLE ONLY SEE WHAT THEY WANT TO SEE

Why Some Perspectives Stay Narrow, and How to Stay Steady When They Do

Over the past twenty-five years in business and life, I've worked with hundreds of people—partners, builders, agents, developers, family, friends and leaders.

Some were brilliant. Some were hardworking. Some were loyal. Some were visionary. Some were genuinely good human beings. But even great people have blind spots.

And that explained how even a few of the most talented partners I ever worked with had one problem that changed everything for me:

They only saw what they wanted to see.

Not what was true or fair. Not what was best for everyone involved. They only saw what benefited them most—financially or socially.

In those moments, I found myself asking difficult questions:

Why do people only see what they want to see?
Where does that kind of tunnel vision come from?
And how does one deal with someone who refuses to look through any angle but theirs?

This chapter is about those experiences—the frustration they created, the clarity they revealed, and the perspective that allowed me to step away without bitterness. Not because the situations were easy, fair, or painless— but because carrying resentment would have kept me tethered to choices that were never mine in the first place.

By choosing perspective over fixation, I was able to release what I couldn't control, protect what mattered most, and move forward with clarity instead of burden. And in doing so, I discovered something essential.

When you stop being held down by the limitations of others, you create the freedom to build more—with greater focus, greater integrity, and greater peace.

WHEN SOMEONE CAN ONLY SEE FROM ONE ANGLE

There were moments in business when I was completely shocked. Partners who had been fair, reasonable, and collaborative suddenly shifted into self-protection mode.

It didn't matter what the facts were or what the agreements said.
It didn't matter how much time, money, or effort I had put in.
It didn't matter how many neutral third parties validated my reasoning.

They only saw one thing:

What benefited them most.

And they couldn't—or wouldn't—look outside that angle.

When someone is locked into a single perspective, you can feel it. They stop listening. They stop considering alternatives. They stop valuing fairness. They stop collaborating. They stop acknowledging shared history.

Their angle narrows until they can only see what makes *them* win. This is one of the most frustrating dynamics in business—and in life.

WHY PEOPLE ONLY SEE WHAT THEY WANT TO SEE

Perspective doesn't just reflect reality. It protects identity.

When someone refuses to see another angle, it's usually because:

1. Their ego is tied to the outcome.
Another angle feels like a threat to their competence, pride, or image.

2. Their self-worth depends on the win.

Losing the deal feels like losing a part of themselves.

3. Their financial stress narrows their lens.

Pressure makes people self-centered, even if they aren't normally that way.

4. Their past experiences taught them scarcity.

They interpret every negotiation as survival.

5. Their narrative requires you to be wrong.

Some people can't allow both perspectives to be valid—they need *their* version to be the *right* version. And when someone's identity is tied to being "right," they don't just sit and let others acknowledge it. They often go a step further.

They talk to others about the situation not because it brings clarity, but because it brings validation.

They tell their side loudly so they don't have to examine it quietly. They repeat their story to reinforce their position. They gather agreement to avoid accountability. They point fingers at others to feel better about their own choices.

It's not malice—it's insecurity. When people haven't built internal stability, they search for external validation. Their need for an audience is a sign that they don't fully believe the story themselves.

Once you see that clearly, you stop taking it personally. You stop defending yourself unnecessarily or trying to convince them of your angle. The reason is simple: Their narrative isn't about you—it's about protecting the version of themselves they feel safest with.

6. They lack the emotional maturity to separate fairness from fear.

When fear speaks, reason disappears.

When someone is locked into one angle, it's rarely about you. It's about what they *need* the moment to mean for themselves.

Understanding this explains the blindness.

THE REALIZATION: THEY WON'T SEE FROM YOUR ANGLE

In both situations I faced, there came a moment when I realized something painful but freeing:

No explanation was going to change anything.

Not because my explanation wasn't good—it was backed by facts and third-party validation.
Not because I hadn't communicated clearly—I had.
Not because the truth wasn't on the table—it was.

They simply weren't willing to see it. And once someone refuses to widen their angle, all argument becomes wasted energy.

That's when I had to make a choice.

Not an emotional or retaliatory choice. Neither was it a pride-driven choice.

It was the Long View choice:

Take the high road and move on.

TAKING THE HIGH ROAD ISN'T WEAKNESS — IT'S WISDOM

When I decided to take the high road, did I want to push back?
Absolutely.
Did I want to prove my point? Of course.
Did I want to force them to see what they were refusing to consider?
Every bit of me did.

But I've learned something over decades of doing business:

You cannot change someone else's agency.

You cannot force someone to grow.
You cannot force someone to be fair.
You cannot force someone to be self-aware.

You cannot force someone to widen their angle.

You cannot force someone to care about the partnership more than their personal gain.

All you can control is your own integrity.

One of the most grounding truths I've learned is this:

"It is what it is."

It's not about being passive or defeated but about being perspective-driven.

It is what it is. People have the right to choose their angle, even if it's destructive—and I have the right to walk away, even if it costs me.

And yes, it did cost me.

Time. Money. Opportunities. Energy. Heartache.

But the long-term damage I avoided? That was far greater.

Choosing clarity over conflict is not weakness. It's stewardship of your future.

THE PARTNERS YOU KEEP ARE THOSE WHO SEE BEYOND THEMSELVES

For every partner who only saw their own angle, I've also worked with partners who were generous, fair, and self-aware—the kind you stay with for decades.

Partners who pause, listen, think beyond themselves, aim for a win-win, widen their angle before reacting, choose the relationship over ego and understand perspective and practice it.

These are the people who make business good. They are the kind you grow and build legacies with.

And they share specific traits worth looking for.

THE QUALITIES YOU SHOULD GRAVITATE TOWARD

If you want strong partnerships—business, relational, or collaborative—look for people who consistently show these qualities:

1. Perspective Awareness

They can see more than one angle without being defensive.

2. Emotional Maturity

They don't let fear, pride, or stress dictate decisions.

3. Shared-Outcome Mindset

They value collective success over personal gain.

4. Accountability

They own mistakes without shifting blame.

5. Curiosity

They ask questions instead of making assumptions.

6. Transparency

They communicate motives, intentions, and expectations clearly.

7. Integrity Under Pressure

They stay fair even when it costs them.

8. Long View Thinking

They make decisions based on what is right, not what is easy.

9. Respect for Agency

They don't control, manipulate, or pressure.

10. Generosity of Interpretation

They assume good intent unless proven otherwise.

People with these qualities don't just make deals easier. They make the burden of life lighter.

WHAT TO DO WHEN YOU REALIZE SOMEONE WON'T SEE FROM YOUR ANGLE

It's inevitable to meet people who are unwilling—or just can't afford—to see from your angle. As established earlier, you can't force them to see or accept your view. So, what do you do?

Here's the solution—the response that protects your peace and your future:

1. Pause before reacting.

Don't fight a wall. Walls don't listen.

2. Accept their angle for what it is.

Not as truth—but as their current limit.

3. Stop trying to convince them.

Your energy is too valuable to waste where it won't be received.

4. Protect your integrity.

Respond in a way your future self will respect.

5. Set boundaries or step away.

Distance is not punishment—it's wisdom.

6. Learn the lesson without carrying the bitterness.

Not every loss is a loss. Some losses are clarity.

7. Choose partners differently next time.

Experience becomes wisdom only when it informs future decisions.

8. Trust that the right people will never require you to shrink your perspective.

Healthy partnerships expand you—they don't trap you.

THE BEAUTIFUL TRUTH

Those difficult partnerships taught me something invaluable:

You can't control other people's angles, but you can control your own.

And when you choose a clear, widened, grounded angle—you win in ways that money and praise can never match.

Perspective doesn't just change how you see people.

It changes who you partner with.
It changes how you respond.
It changes what you carry.
It changes what you build.

Clarity doesn't just shape your decisions—it shapes your entire future.

SIDE QUEST 4: "The Blueprint Scan"

Tagline: Find the hidden rules running your reactions.

Action Steps:

1. Answer these:

   - "What did I learn growing up about conflict?"
   - "What emotions do I default to under pressure?"
   - "Where did I learn that from?"

2. Write what your blueprint *makes you assume*.
3. Label each assumption as:

   - Helpful
   - Harmful
   - Outdated

Outcome: Clarity about unconscious emotional patterns and their origins.

SIDE QUEST 5: "The Reaction Rewrite"

Tagline: Give the past you a better script.

Action Steps:

1. Recall a moment where your reaction surprised you.
2. Write the reaction you had.
3. Write the emotion that caused it.
4. Rewrite the reaction as the grounded version of you.

Outcome: Rewires the emotional "autopilot."

SIDE QUEST 6: "The Hidden Load Inventory"

Tagline: Identify what you're carrying that no one sees.

Action Steps:

1. List the emotional burdens you're carrying right now.
2. Put a star next to the ones no one knows about.
3. Circle the one that affects your interpretation the most.
4. Share ONE item with someone safe.

Outcome: Emotional weight-reduction through awareness + expression.

SIDE QUEST 7: "Untying The Rope"

Releasing What Was Never Yours to Carry

This side quest is not about fixing the past. It's about **untying yourself from it**.

Some frustrations linger not because they're unresolved, but because you're still emotionally tethered to someone else's choices. This exercise helps you identify where that tether exists— and consciously release it.

Step 1: Name the Tether

Think of one situation where someone else's perspective, decision, or behavior affected you deeply.

Answer honestly:

- What did they choose?
- How did their choice limit, hurt, or cost you?
- What part of that situation are you still carrying?

Write it plainly. No justification. No softening.

"I'm still carrying ___________."

Step 2: Separate Responsibility from Impact

There is a critical distinction in this book: **Impact does not equal responsibility.**

Ask yourself:

- What part of this situation was actually *mine*?
- What part belonged to *them*?
- What am I still trying to control that was never in my agency?

Write two short lists:

- What was mine to own
- What was never mine to fix

That's where clarity begins.

Step 3: Identify the Hidden Cost of Holding On

Resentment always charges interest.

Ask yourself:

- What is this resentment costing me *today*?
- How does it show up in my thinking, energy, or focus?
- What does it quietly steal from my future?

Be specific. The goal is awareness—not self-criticism.

Step 4: Choose Perspective Over Fixation

Read this sentence slowly, then complete it:

"If I released this fully, I would gain __________."

Then ask:

- What would I build with that regained energy?
- Where would my attention go instead?
- Who would I become if this no longer defined me?

Perspective is not denial; it's **direction**.

Step 5: The Letting-Go Statement

Repeat this sentence and write it somewhere visible for the next week:

"I release what I could not control, and I choose to move forward with clarity instead of weight."

You don't need to feel ready. You just need to choose intentionally.

Final Reflection

Letting go doesn't mean:

- They were right
- It didn't hurt
- It didn't matter

It means you are no longer allowing someone else's limitations to determine the size of your future.

That is not weakness. It is **freedom with clarity.**

PART III
UNDERSTANDING OTHERS

CHAPTER 12

THE EMOTIONAL HORIZON

Reading Your Emotions Before They Rewrite the Story

"When emotion rises, perspective narrows. Your job is to widen the frame before you decide."

Every person lives with an *emotional horizon*—a point where their capacity thins, their patience shortens, and their clarity shrinks into a tight, foggy circle.

Most conflicts don't happen because people don't care. They happen because people hit their emotional horizon without realizing it.

You know what it feels like when:

- You're patient … until you're not.
- You're understanding … until you're not.
- You're calm … until you're not.
- You're present … until something inside you snaps.

That snap isn't failure. It isn't immaturity or evidence that something is "wrong" with you.

It's a signal.

A warning light. A sign that your emotional horizon has tightened.

EMOTIONAL CAPACITY IS LIKE WEATHER

Your emotional horizon shifts day by day, just like the sky.

On some days, your emotional sky is wide and open:

You can handle stress, surprises, setbacks, and misunderstandings with grace.

You interpret generously.

You stay grounded.

On some days, the sky clouds over:

Your patience thins.

Your reactions sharpen.

Your bandwidth shrinks.

And on some other days, the storm rolls in:

Old wounds flare.

Stress piles high.

Fatigue amplifies everything.

And the smallest inconvenience becomes the spark that lights the whole fuse.

Your emotional horizon is shaped by:

- sleep
- stress
- workload
- relational tension
- unresolved emotions
- personal disappointment
- financial pressure
- physical health
- mental load
- internal narrative

When someone reacts strongly, the reaction is rarely about you. It's about the horizon they're standing in.

THE HIDDEN COST OF PILED EMOTIONS

The Backpack You Don't Remember Packing

I want you to imagine something.

You wake up one morning and put on a backpack. It feels light, barely noticeable. Then you go about your day.

At some point, someone brushes past you and quietly drops a small stone inside. You don't see it happen. You don't hear it.

All you feel is a slight shift in weight. No big deal.

Later, another stone goes in.

Then another.

A comment that stung a little.
A responsibility you didn't ask for.
A disappointment you never addressed.
A misunderstanding you swallowed instead of clarified.
A frustration you told yourself you'd deal with later.

Each one is small. Each one feels manageable. So, you keep walking.

Hours turn into days. Days turn into weeks. And somewhere along the way, your posture changes.

You walk slower. Your shoulders tighten. Your patience shortens. Your emotional horizon narrows.

But here's the strange part: You don't remember putting anything in the backpack.

So you're left without an explanation when someone asks why you're tense, why your fuse seems short, why small things feel heavy, or why you react faster than you used to.

You just know you feel tired.

HOW EMOTIONAL LOAD IS REALLY CREATED

Most emotional weight isn't caused by one big event.

It's created by **accumulation**.

The stones didn't get into the backpack at once, it was gradual.

These stones might be:

- assumptions you never corrected
- feelings you didn't name
- boundaries you didn't set
- interpretations you didn't question
- moments you carried alone

No single stone breaks you. But together, they change how you move through the world.

And the most dangerous part? The load becomes *normal*. You forget what it felt like to walk without it.

WHY YOUR EMOTIONAL HORIZON SHRINKS

As the backpack gets heavier, something subtle happens. You stop seeing far.

When you're carrying emotional weight:

- neutral comments feel sharp
- small setbacks feel personal
- inconveniences feel like threats
- conversations feel draining
- patience feels expensive

Your emotional horizon shortens not because you're weak, but because you're overloaded.

Perspective requires space—and emotional weight collapses that space.

THE MOMENT YOU REALIZE THE BAG ISN'T EMPTY

There usually comes a moment when:

A reaction surprises you.

A comment hits harder than it should.

A small conflict feels overwhelming.

You snap when you normally wouldn't.

It's not a character flaw because it's not your *usual*.

That's your body and mind saying, *"You're carrying more than you think."*

And here's the most important realization: No one else knows what's in your backpack. **And most of them didn't mean to add weight**.

They just didn't know you never took anything out.

THE WORK ISN'T STOPPING THE STONES

It's emptying the bag

You can't control whether people drop stones. Life will always add weight.

The work of perspective is to help you:

- notice when the load is increasing
- name what you're carrying
- question which stones belong to you
- intentionally set some down

Some stones are lessons.
Some are grief.
Some are responsibility.
Some are misunderstandings that need clarification.
Some are resentments that need release.

But you shouldn't be carrying any of them unconsciously or unintentionally.

WHAT HAPPENS WHEN YOU START UNLOADING

When you begin to empty the backpack, it gets lighter and:

your posture straightens

your breathing deepens

your reactions soften

your horizon widens

Not because life got easier—but because **you stopped carrying everything silently**.

Perspective doesn't remove weight from life. It teaches you how to carry only what matters.

THE QUIET TRUTH OF THE EMOTIONAL HORIZON

Your emotional horizon isn't limited by who you are. It's limited by what you're carrying. The moment you realize that, you don't just feel lighter, you see farther.

One small frustration doesn't change much. But dozens of small frustrations … stacked quietly, unnoticed … turn into emotional overload.

People don't break because of one big moment.

They break because of a thousand small ones they never acknowledged.

Stress compounds. Fear compounds. Guilt compounds. Unspoken emotions compound.

And, eventually, the horizon disappears beneath the weight.

THE MOMENT I HIT MY HORIZON

(The Backpack I Didn't Know I Was Carrying)

There was a time in Kansas City when everything in the sales organization I managed collided at once.

Targets were looming. Two deals that should've closed stalled at the last minute. A key rep missed a follow-up that mattered; another was frustrated about commission timing. A client pushed back harder than expected. Forecast calls stacked up. Texts didn't stop. Phones rang. Pressure crept higher.

None of it was catastrophic. This was sales, I knew that. It was leadership. It was normal.

But internally, something was tightening.

My shoulders stayed tense. My thoughts kept sprinting ahead to what could go wrong next. Each new issue felt heavier than it should have.

That's because, without realizing it, I had been letting people place rocks in my backpack all week long.

Each conversation added one.
Each expectation added another.

Each responsibility I absorbed without pausing added weight. Each frustration I carried silently slipped another rock inside.

No single rock mattered much. But by the end of the week, the pack was full.

And here's the part most people miss: The backpack doesn't announce itself as it becomes full.

It doesn't come with a warning label. It just slowly pulls your posture forward, shortens your patience, and narrows your emotional horizon.

By Friday, I wasn't responding to the moment anymore. I was reacting to the weight.

Sitting alone in my truck after work, I finally noticed it. Nothing that week had broken me. But everything had been added to my backpack day by day.

That's when the clarity hit:

Your emotional horizon collapses not because of one heavy moment, but because of too many unacknowledged ones.

I hadn't failed as a leader. I hadn't lost my edge or become less capable.

I had just forgotten to set the backpack down. That realization changed how I led. Awareness is how you unzip the pack, take inventory, and regain your balance. When you do that, your emotional horizon widens again.

The week didn't change and the pressure didn't disappear. But I changed—because I finally noticed the backpack I'd been carrying all along.

THE THREE EMOTIONAL HORIZONS

Everyone operates in one of three different horizons.

1. The Wide Horizon

This is your strongest emotional state. You're steady, patient, and grounded.

You:

- interpret generously
- communicate clearly
- listen without defensiveness
- respond instead of react
- see the bigger picture

Wide horizons produce clarity.

2. The Narrow Horizon

You can still function—but you're stretched thin.

You:

- react faster
- interpret more personally
- assume more
- lose patience quicker
- feel tension rise in your body

Narrow horizons create miscommunication.

3. The Foggy Horizon

You're emotionally overloaded.

You:

- feel overwhelmed
- lose objectivity
- think in extremes
- take everything personally
- struggle to separate old pain from new moments

Foggy horizons produce conflict—every single time.

Of course, most relationships break down not in the wide horizon, **but in the narrow and foggy ones.**

HEALTHY PEOPLE COMMUNICATE THEIR HORIZON

Emotionally mature people say things like:

- "I'm overwhelmed—can we talk in an hour?"
- "I'm feeling sensitive today. It's not you, just where I'm at."
- "My stress is high—let me reset before we continue."
- "I want to get this right. I need a moment to breathe."

This is not avoidance; it is stewardship. It is taking responsibility for your emotional lens *before* it distorts the moment.

80% of avoidable conflict disappears simply by naming your horizon.

HELPING OTHERS NAVIGATE THEIR HORIZON

Perspective means recognizing the horizon someone else is standing in.

- Silence might be overwhelming exhaustion.
- A sharp tone might be fatigue.
- Withdrawal might be emotional overload.
- Defensiveness might be fear.
- Irritation might be pressure.

Most emotional reactions are responses to internal weight—not external events.

When you see someone's horizon, you stop reacting to their behavior and start responding to their condition.

That's emotional intelligence. It's perspective in action.

QUESTIONS THAT WIDEN YOUR HORIZON

Ask yourself:

- "What am I carrying that no one sees?"
- "What stress is shaping my interpretation?"
- "What assumption did I jump to?"
- "What emotion is speaking louder than truth?"
- "What would this look like if I zoomed out?"

Perspective isn't the absence of emotion.

Perspective is emotion aligned with truth.

CHAPTER 13

CLARITY IN CONFLICT

The Perspective Shift That Turns Arguments Into Understanding

Most people fear conflict because they only know two forms:

Explosive Conflict

Where emotions erupt and damage relationships.

Avoidant Conflict

Where issues are buried and resentment grows in silence.

But conflict itself isn't the problem, **confusion is.**

When conflict lacks clarity, it becomes chaotic. However, when conflict is full of clarity, it becomes productive.

Healthy conflict is, in simple terms, **two perspectives seeking alignment without losing dignity.**

THE THREE LAYERS OF EVERY CONFLICT

Every conflict has three layers:

1. The Surface Issue

This is the event. It could be:

- what was said
- what was done
- what was missed
- what triggered the irritation

This is the *least* important layer.

2. The Interpretation

This is what each person *believed* the moment meant.

It is precisely where conflict lives.

3. The Emotional Charge

This is what the moment activated. It might be:

- fear
- shame
- insecurity
- disappointment
- frustration
- feeling unseen

This is the layer most people ignore. Ironically, it's the layer that must be understood to resolve conflict.

THE 80/20 RULE OF CONFLICT

80% of conflict is emotional interpretation; 20% is the actual issue.

Fix the 80%, and the 20% resolves itself.

A CONSTRUCTION CONFLICT

A subcontractor once missed a deadline and it made the project manager react strongly.

Voices rose and tension escalated.

But when we broke it down, it wasn't all about the missed deadline.

The surface issue:

A delivery was late.

The interpretation:

- The project manager interpreted the delay as disrespect.
- The subcontractor interpreted the reaction as unfair pressure.

The emotional charge:

- The project manager felt the weight of responsibility.
- The subcontractor felt the fear of being blamed.

Once these layers were identified, the conflict dissolved. The conflict wasn't the issue—**the interpretation was.**

THE SIMPLE STRUCTURE OF HEALTHY CONFLICT

Healthy conflict requires three elements:

1. Clarify Intent

Misunderstanding fuels conflict. So it goes without saying that, clarifying one's intent dissolves it.

- "I wasn't trying to attack you."
- "I wasn't dismissing you."
- "I wasn't ignoring you."

When intent is clarified, hearts soften.

2. Clarify Impact

Good intentions don't erase negative impact.

- "I see how my tone landed wrong."
- "I understand that this felt unfair."
- "I get how that could have hurt you."

Impact matters as much as intention.

3. Clarify the Path Forward

Conflict without direction creates resentment.

- "Next time, let's slow down and explain the context."
- "I'll communicate earlier."
- "Let's check in before reacting."

Clarity prevents repetition.

THE FOUR RULES OF CLARITY-BASED CONFLICT

1. Stay on the issue at hand—don't stack old ones.
2. Use specific examples—avoid "always" or "never."
3. Speak from experience, not accusation:

   - "I felt…" instead of "You made me…"

4. Pause when emotion outruns clarity.

   If clarity drops, stop and reset.

CONFLICT DOESN'T BREAK RELATIONSHIPS —AVOIDANCE DOES

Avoidance creates:

- resentment
- assumption
- emotional distance
- quiet frustration

Avoidance is silent corrosion. Clarity is repair.

WHAT CLARITY SOUNDS LIKE

- "Help me understand what you heard."
- "What part felt the hardest for you?"
- "What were you expecting from me?"
- "What do you need to feel resolved?"
- "Here's what I meant—and here's what I missed."

Clarity invites honesty—**without punishment.**

CHAPTER 14

SEEING THE LONG GAME

Choosing Who You're Becoming Over What You're Feeling

Perspective is long-game vision.

It's the ability to look past the moment you're in—the emotion you're feeling, the frustration rising, the discomfort pulling you inward—and see the future you are quietly building with every reaction, every word, and every choice.

Short-term perspective asks, "How do I feel right now?"

Long-term perspective asks, "Who am I becoming because of what I choose right now?"

This single shift is the difference between:

- families that grow stronger vs. families that fracture
- leaders who inspire trust vs. leaders who create fear
- couples who deepen connection vs. couples who drift apart
- individuals who heal vs. individuals who repeat the same cycle

The long game isn't complicated. It's simply harder than reacting to the moment.

THE POWER OF DELAYED INTERPRETATION

Short-term interpretation reacts while long-term interpretation reflects.

When something triggers you, your emotional lens shrinks. Your brain tries to interpret quickly, and quick interpretations are, in most cases, narrow interpretations.

Short-term vision says:

- "This is terrible."

- "They're being difficult."
- "I need to defend myself."
- "I need to fix this right now."

Long-term vision says:

- "There might be something here I'm supposed to learn."
- "They might be afraid, overloaded, or hurting."
- "Let me listen before I assume."
- "The relationship is more important than the moment."

Long-term thinking isn't passive. It's disciplined.

THE STRUGGLING TEAM MEMBER

Years ago, I had a young team member who struggled in his first few months. He made mistakes that slowed us down. He missed details and communicated poorly under pressure. A few people quietly suggested letting him go.

Everything in me wanted efficiency—the short-term fix. But something nudged me to look deeper.

Then I saw the deeper truth.

He didn't need replacement.
He needed mentorship.
He needed structure.
He needed someone to see the long-game potential in him instead of the short-term frustration.

So I slowed down. I invested and coached. I looked past the rocky beginning and saw the man he could become.

Today, he's successful and has the confidence to make his own choices for the benefit of the team. Short-term judgment would have written him off. Long-term perspective revealed who he truly was becoming.

This is the gift of long-game vision: **You see people not as they are, but as they can be with time and support.**

LONG-GAME THINKING IN RELATIONSHIPS

Short-term thinking tries to 'win' disagreements; long-term thinking tries to understand.

Short-term thinking reacts to tone; long-term thinking listens for what the tone is protecting.

Short-term thinking protects pride; long-term thinking protects the relationship.

Short-term thinking asks, "How do I make this moment feel better?"

Long-term thinking asks, "How do we make this relationship stronger?"

Choosing the long game means choosing maturity over urgency.

THE HABIT OF ASKING FUTURE-FOCUSED QUESTIONS

Here are questions that instantly shift you from impulse to intention:

- "Will this matter in five days? Five months? Five years?"
- "Is my reaction aligned with who I want to be?"
- "Is this about the moment or about a deeper meaning?"
- "Is this protecting my pride or protecting our connection?"
- "If my kids were watching, would I be proud of this version of me?"
- "What does the future version of me wish I'd say right now?"

These questions widen your emotional horizon and anchor you in wisdom rather than reaction.

Long-game perspective doesn't make life easier—it makes life richer.

CHAPTER 15

BUILDING A LIFE OF PERSPECTIVE

Creating Environments Where Understanding Thrives

Perspective is not a technique you turn on during conflict.

It's a way of living—a steady, grounded posture that reshapes how you speak, listen, work, love, lead, parent, and grow.

A life built on perspective sees:

- deeper than emotion
- wider than the moment
- farther than frustration
- clearer than conflict
- truer than fear

Perspective doesn't remove struggles—it simply keeps the struggle from ruling you.

THE THREE FOUNDATIONS OF A PERSPECTIVE-DRIVEN LIFE

Every perspective-rich life is built on three pillars: emotional awareness, relational understanding, and future-focused vision.

These pillars create environments where connection grows naturally and misunderstanding has less room to thrive.

1. Emotional Awareness

Emotional awareness is knowing what's happening inside you before your reactions speak for you.

It is the ability to:

- name your emotional horizon
- recognize when old wounds hijack current moments
- pause instead of react
- separate present reality from past memories
- notice when your lens has narrowed

Emotion isn't the enemy; unexamined emotion is. Emotionally aware people don't avoid emotion; they learn how to carry it well.

2. Relational Understanding

Relational understanding is the ability to see the invisible blueprint others are living from.

It means:

- listening for meaning, not just words
- noticing emotional cues
- repairing quickly instead of defending slowly
- interpreting generously
- assuming less and asking more
- speaking with clarity instead of expectation

When you understand someone's blueprint, you stop taking them personally—and start seeing them compassionately.

3. Future-Focused Vision

Future-focused vision is the discipline of letting your values guide your reactions instead of your emotions.

It is:

- choosing the high road even when the low road is tempting
- responding with intention rather than impulse
- thinking long-term in short-term moments
- investing in the kind of relationships you want to have
- becoming the person your future needs

Future-focused vision creates internal stability. It anchors you in who you're becoming, not just who you've been or what you feel like in the moment.

AREAS WHERE PERSPECTIVE TRANSFORMS LIFE

Perspective quietly upgrades every part of your world:

- Relationships → deeper connection, easier repair
- Leadership → calm authority instead of reactive pressure
- Family → emotional safety and support
- Teams → unity, trust, and clarity
- Self-growth → maturity rooted in awareness
- Conflict → understanding instead of explosions

Perspective makes life lighter because you stop carrying unnecessary interpretations and start carrying wisdom instead.

CHAPTER 16

BUILDING CONFIDENCE THROUGH BELIEF

How Perspective Shapes Growth, Confidence, and the Way People Rise

Some of the most powerful lessons in perspective don't come from boardrooms, conflict, or relationships—they come from watching nine-year-olds play soccer.

When our oldest daughter was nine, she wanted to play. I had played for many years, so I volunteered to help coach. I thought I was stepping into a sport. But I was stepping into a masterclass on human behavior.

What I learned on that field over the next 10 years reshaped the way I lead, the way I parent, the way I communicate, and the way I interpret people.

When you put a group of kids on a field and ask them to work together, respond to pressure, recover from mistakes, and trust their own instincts—you get a front-row seat to the impact of perspective.

And you learn quickly that:

People don't grow in environments of fear; they grow in environments of belief.

THE FIRST LESSON: THEY ALREADY KNOW WHEN THEY MESS UP

I learned early that the girls didn't need me to point out their mistakes. They already knew.

When a pass went the wrong direction, when a shot sailed too wide, when they lost the ball on a dribble, or they hesitated instead of shooting, I didn't have to tell them.

I didn't have to say a word. It was clear in the way their shoulders dropped. In the way their eyes flickered with embarrassment and their pace slowed for a moment. Nobody else needed to tell me they felt it.

Kids are more emotionally aware than we give them credit for. They don't need criticism to recognize an error—they need courage to recover from it.

Furthermore, criticism doesn't build courage. **Perspective does.**

THE SECOND LESSON: CRITICISM SHRINKS — ENCOURAGEMENT EXPANDS

I saw quickly that when I reacted with frustration, they tightened up. They hesitated. They played smaller. They became afraid of the ball—not because they lacked skill, but because they feared disappointing me.

Criticism narrows perspective. It collapses emotional horizon and turns every decision into a moment of survival.

But when I coached through encouragement—"That's okay, get it next time," "You're seeing the right idea," "Great effort—keep going," "Reset. You've got another chance"— something different happened.

Their perspective opened.
Their confidence rose.
Their effort increased.
Their joy returned.
Their performance improved.

They didn't just play harder, they played freer.

Why?

Because encouragement widens emotional horizon. Encouragement tells someone, "You're safe to try again."

And people who feel safe … rise.

THE THIRD LESSON: PEOPLE PERFORM BETTER WHEN THEY FEEL SEEN, NOT SCARED

Over the years, I coached multiple teams. The ages, leagues, and skill levels were different. But the pattern was the same:

Players who felt *seen* grew. Players who felt *scared* shrank.

I watched other coaches operate from the opposite lens—yelling, critiquing, and erupting at every mistake. Their players played tight, uncertain, anxious. They regressed over time, not because they lacked talent, but because fear consumed the emotional space where confidence was supposed to live.

When people are encouraged, they feel seen and understood. They lose the fear of failing because they know they are seen beyond their current performance.

Fear builds compliance while encouragement builds growth.

Fear creates short-term effort while encouragement creates long-term development.

Fear produces players who avoid mistakes while encouragement produces players who take opportunities.

And the deeper lesson is this:

The way someone interprets your presence shapes how they perform around you.

THE FOURTH LESSON: PEOPLE SHOW UP DIFFERENTLY WHEN THEY BELIEVE THEY CAN

Over the years, many of the girls I coached went on to play at a higher level.

They didn't get there because of me. It was not because of drills or coaching systems.

They advanced because they believed they could. They internalized confidence, trusted their instincts, and saw possibility instead of pressure.

Skill matters.

Talent matters.

Training matters.

But, belief?

Belief is the engine.

Perspective builds belief. Encouragement expands it, clarity reinforces it, and steady leadership protects it.

Belief shapes identity, especially in young people.

THE FIFTH LESSON: DIFFERENT ANGLES REQUIRE DIFFERENT APPROACHES

Every player had a different temperament.

Some needed reassurance.

Some needed structure.

Some needed space.

Some needed detailed instruction.

Some needed freedom to create.

Some needed to talk through mistakes.

Some needed a quick reset and a pat on the back.

Same team, same sport, same coach. But different angles.

And perspective taught me something essential:

You can't coach everyone the same way because not everyone sees from the same place.

Leadership requires adjusting your approach—not your standards, not your expectations, not your values—but your angle.

The same is true in marriages, friendships, workplaces, and families.

Perspective makes you flexible without losing your clarity.

THE SIXTH LESSON: SUPPORT CREATES EFFORT — AND THEN IT CREATES LEADERSHIP

Something remarkable happened each season.

The more positive and steady the environment became, the harder the players worked.

Apparently, encouragement didn't make them lax. It made them motivated. Similarly, support didn't lower standards, it raised performance.

When the kids felt believed in, they pushed themselves. But when they felt criticized, they held back.

But the real breakthrough came later, when they didn't just receive support—**they started giving it.**

Once the players learned how to stay positive themselves, they naturally began encouraging each other:

"Shake it off—you've got it."
"Great try, keep going."
"You're in the right spot."
"We'll get the next one."

They celebrated each other's wins, pulled each other out of low moments, stayed connected even under pressure, and became a team that lifted itself.

That is the big win.

As a coach, that's the moment you hope for—when the culture no longer comes *from you*, but *through them.* Because a team that supports each other becomes self-led, self-motivated, self-accountable, and consequently, unstoppable.

This is true far beyond sports: People rise higher when the people beside them rise too.

Encouragement doesn't replace accountability—it creates a culture where accountability thrives.

THE LEADERSHIP TRUTH THE FIELD TAUGHT ME

Here's the part that aligns perfectly with the heart of this book:

People don't grow because you pressure them. They grow because you see them.

Pressure distorts perspective.
Criticism narrows emotional horizon.
Fear shuts down potential.

But clarity, encouragement, steady presence, and perspective open the internal space where growth happens.

The soccer field just gave me a front-row seat to a lesson life had been trying to teach all along:

What you see in people often becomes what they see in themselves.

THE TAKEAWAY FOR REAL LIFE

The soccer seasons ended, but the lessons didn't.

The same principles apply everywhere:

- Your kids
- Your spouse
- Your employees
- Your partners
- Your friends
- Yourself

People perform better when they feel safe to grow; they become more confident when someone else believes in them; and they rise when perspective widens the emotional horizon around them. Conversely, the only direction people move when led through fear is backward.

Perspective isn't just something that helps you interpret others. It's something that helps others rise through how you interpret them.

THE FINAL WHISTLE

Coaching taught me this:

Encouragement is not soft.

It's strategic.

It is emotional leadership at its highest level.

And the most life-changing part?

You don't need a field, a team, or a whistle to use it.

Every day, with every person in your life, you have a choice: Shrink their confidence through criticism or strengthen their identity through perspective. What you choose changes more than the moment; it changes the person.

And sometimes, the greatest victories in life don't come from winning games. They come from helping people see who they can become.

SIDE QUEST 8: "The Trust Beam Check"

Tagline: Reinforce the structure before it cracks.

Action Steps:

1. Identify one relationship with a "hairline crack."
2. Ask yourself:

   - "What caused the gap?"
   - "What part did I play?"
   - "What would rebuild the frame?"
3. Take ONE action:

   - Text of appreciation
   - Apology
   - Clear commitment
   - Clarifying conversation

Outcome: Stronger relational trust through proactive repair.

SIDE QUEST 9: "The Two Rooms Exercise"

Tagline: Different rooms. Same foundation.

Action Steps:

1. Draw a house with two rooms.
2. Label one room *your* emotional needs.
3. Label the other room *their* emotional needs.
4. Draw one shared foundation underneath labeled: **"What matters to both of us."**
5. Fill in the shared values.

Outcome: Visual clarity that different needs don't equal distance.

SIDE QUEST 10: "The Clarifying Conversation"

Tagline: Solve the misunderstanding, not the argument.

Action Steps:

Have a conversation with someone using ONLY these four questions:

1. "What did you hear me say?"
2. "What did you mean in that moment?"
3. "What part felt off to you?"
4. "What do you need from me going forward?"

Outcome: Learning to stay emotionally regulated during conflict.

SIDE QUEST 11: "Coaching Without A Whistle"

Practicing the Perspective That Helps People Rise

You don't need a field, a team, or a jersey to be a coach. You are already coaching—every day—through how you interpret people and respond to their effort.

This side quest is about becoming intentional with that influence.

STEP 1: IDENTIFY WHO YOU'RE COACHING (EVEN IF YOU DON'T CALL IT THAT)

Write down the names of 2–3 people you regularly interact with where your response carries weight:

- A child
- A spouse or partner
- An employee or coworker
- A business partner
- A friend
- Yourself

Next to each name, answer this honestly:

When they make a mistake around me, do they tighten up—or lean in?

Write here: ____

STEP 2: NOTICE YOUR DEFAULT COACHING LENS

Think about the last time one of these people struggled, missed something, or fell short.

Ask yourself:

- Did I respond from correction or connection?
- Was my tone focused on the mistake—or the recovery?
- Did my response shrink their confidence or widen it?

Write down one real example:

STEP 3: PRACTICE THE "RESET RESPONSE"

The next time someone makes a mistake in front of you, pause and use one of these **reset responses** instead of criticism:

- "That's okay—what did you notice?"
- "You're seeing the right thing. Try again."
- "What would you do differently next time?"
- "I believe in you—keep going."
- "Shake it off. You've got another chance."

Your goal is not to ignore standards—it's to protect belief while reinforcing growth.

Which phrase feels most natural for you?

STEP 4: WATCH WHAT CHANGES

Over the next week, pay attention to what happens when you shift your response:

- Do they try again faster?
- Do they speak up more?
- Do they take more initiative?
- Do they recover quicker from mistakes?
- Do they begin encouraging themselves—or others?

Write down what you notice:

STEP 5: COACH YOURSELF THE SAME WAY

This is the most overlooked part.

The way you coach others is often the way you speak to yourself.

Ask:

- When I mess up, do I criticize or encourage myself?
- Do I shrink after mistakes—or reset and re-engage?
- Am I building fear in myself—or belief?

Rewrite one recent self-critical thought into a **coach's voice**:

- Old thought: _______________________________________
- New perspective: ___________________________________

THE POINT OF THE SIDE QUEST

You don't build confidence by demanding perfection. You build it by creating a safe place to try again.

And the real win—just like on the field—comes when:

- People start encouraging themselves.
- People start supporting each other.
- The culture no longer depends on you alone.

That's when you know you're coaching well.

Remember, **what you see in people often becomes what they see in themselves**.

Carry that lens with you and watch how people rise.

PART IV
BECOMING STEADY

CHAPTER 17

THE TURNING POINT OF SELF-UNDERSTANDING

Why Your Inner Clarity Shapes Every Outer Outcome

Every journey toward clarity eventually reaches a crossroads—a moment where the way you've always seen yourself no longer matches the person you're becoming.

It doesn't arrive with fanfare. Most people don't even recognize it while it's happening.

But later—sometimes months or years later—they look back and say:

"That was the moment everything shifted."

Not because life suddenly got easier or the world changed, but because **they** changed.

This chapter is about *that* shift—the inner turning point where perspective stops being a tool you use occasionally and becomes a lens that shapes who you are.

It is the moment when:

- you stop reacting automatically;
- you stop interpreting yourself through old stories;
- you stop carrying the weight of someone else's blueprint;
- you stop living as the "past you;"
- and begin stepping into a steadier, wiser version of yourself.

This is the turning point of self-understanding—**the moment where clarity becomes identity.**

THE MOMENT YOU REALIZE YOU'RE NOT WHO YOU USED TO BE

I remember a moment on a jobsite. It was an ordinary moment that was neither dramatic nor life-changing on the surface. But something in me shifted so clearly that I still think about it.

The sun was dropping behind the ridge and the crew was wrapping up. One of my guys rushed over, frustrated and overwhelmed. His voice was sharp, his tone was tense, and his emotions were high.

Years earlier, I would've matched that energy. I would've reacted emotionally. I would've taken his intensity personally. I would've risen to his level rather than staying grounded in mine. But this time, something was different.

As he talked, I could *see* his stress. I could *hear* the panic under his words. I could *feel* the pressure he was carrying.

So, instead of absorbing it, I stayed steady. Calm. Clear. Present.

Not because the issue didn't matter, but because *something in me had shifted*.

Perspective had become my default. It wasn't something I had to *do*.

I wasn't performing calmness—I *was* calm.
I wasn't forcing clarity—I *had* clarity.
I wasn't pretending to be grounded—I *was* grounded.

In that moment, I learned something:

Growth isn't when you learn something new. Growth is when you become someone new.

SELF-UNDERSTANDING IS A SERIES OF SMALL AWAKENINGS

People imagine self-understanding as one big breakthrough—one giant moment where everything suddenly makes sense. Well, it's not like that.

Identity shifts in small ways. You realize the shift when:

- you communicate differently

- you handle conflict with more patience
- you stop taking things personally
- you interpret more generously
- you pause before reacting
- you listen with curiosity instead of defensiveness
- you speak from clarity instead of insecurity
- you stop needing to 'win' to feel secure

These tiny shifts stack up until one day, you realize:

You're not living from your old blueprint anymore.

You've quietly become someone steadier, calmer, more grounded.

Growth happens quietly—and then it announces itself loudly through your (better) choices.

NEW IDENTITY, NEW LENS

Most people never reach this turning point because they still interpret themselves through old lenses:

- old mistakes
- old labels
- old insecurities
- old fears
- old roles
- old emotional patterns
- old versions of themselves

Your past interprets your present until you update the lens.

You cannot build a new identity using old language. You cannot build a steady future using unstable interpretations. You cannot step into confidence while holding onto stories that shake you.

One of the greatest shifts in self-understanding is realizing this:

I am not obligated to remain the person I was before I knew what I know now.

Read that again.

It's the doorway to emotional freedom.

THE MID- CONSTRUCTION CHAOS

There is something I learned from framing houses with my dad when I was younger.

When framing a house, there is a stage where everything looks chaotic. You see boards everywhere, temporary supports, open spaces, exposed beams, and scattered tools. It looks nothing like a finished home.

Homeowners walk through and say, "I can't see it yet."

And I always tell them, "You're not supposed to—it's not done becoming what it's meant to be."

The same is true for you.

There are seasons when your internal growth looks messy:

- you're learning new patterns but still reacting in old ways
- you're gaining clarity but still tripping over past wounds
- you're becoming grounded but still losing your footing occasionally
- you're improving communication but still catching yourself using old habits

This isn't failure. This is **framing**.

Your identity is mid-construction. A work-in-progress. It's still messy; in it's temporary, essential state. It's not a stage to run from or just skip because it's a part of the process. Since shifts don't just happen at once, this seemingly chaotic season is inevitable.

It's not proof that you're hopeless; it's a sign that you're shedding old weight.

So, don't be afraid to navigate the chaos. Just like the framing of a construction in progress, focus on what the result will look like and not what the process currently looks like.

You are not finished or hopeless—you are becoming.

THE TURNING POINT

Before you even realize you've reached the turning point, three shifts begin inside you. You may already be in one of them right now.

SHIFT 1: You Become Aware of Your Patterns Instead of Controlled by Them

Before this shift, your patterns feel like "just who you are". You might have been used to:

- snapping under stress
- shutting down when misunderstood
- defending before listening
- taking tone personally
- assuming the worst
- reading between lines that aren't there

However, after the shift, something changes. You begin to notice the pattern *as it happens*. You start to understand things like:

- "That's my old blueprint talking."
- "This reaction is about my past, not this moment."
- "I'm interpreting this through insecurity."
- "I'm slipping into my old angle."

Awareness is not the finish line—but it is the first doorway.

SHIFT 2: You Separate Your Feelings From Your Identity

This is one of the biggest markers of emotional maturity.

Before the shift:

If you felt insecure → you *were* insecure.
If you felt overwhelmed → you *were* overwhelmed.
If you felt misunderstood → you *were* misunderstood.

After the shift, you begin saying:

- "I'm feeling this—but this isn't who I am."
- "This emotion is loud—but it's not the truth."

- "This moment is triggering—but I don't have to interpret it through fear."

This shift is the beginning of emotional mastery.

SHIFT 3: You Choose Responses Based on Clarity, Not Survival

Before this shift, everything feels personal, urgent, threatening.

After this shift:

- you slow reactions
- you interpret more generously
- you don't jump to conclusions
- you ask better questions
- you respond from steadiness instead of fear
- you choose words from intention, not emotion

Your old identity was shaped by survival. Your new identity is shaped by clarity.

This is the turning point of self-understanding.

THE OLD SELF DOESN'T DISAPPEAR — IT QUIETS

A common misconception is that once you grow, your old patterns vanish.

But no, they don't vanish. They simply lose power.

Your old self still whispers:

- "You're not enough."
- "They don't understand you."
- "You're messing everything up."
- "This conflict means danger."

But the difference is that those whispers no longer drive the car.

Your new self takes the wheel while your old self becomes mere commentary. Your new self becomes direction.

And after long periods of you not acting on it, the old voice grows quiet.

THREE QUESTIONS OF CHANGE

At this turning point, your inner dialogue changes.

These three simple questions open doors to deeper clarity:

1. "What part of me is speaking right now?"

Is it the:

- child in me?
- overwhelmed me?
- defensive me?
- old me?
- steady me?

Naming the voice gives you power over it.

2. "Is this reaction about now or about my past?"

Most emotional reactions are echoes from old wounds.

This question stops old pain from hijacking new moments.

3. "What would the steady version of me do right now?"

This question instantly widens your perspective.

It helps you respond from clarity, not from conditioning.

THE TURNING POINT ISN'T PERFECTION — IT'S OWNERSHIP

Self-understanding doesn't mean:

- you never lose perspective
- you never get triggered
- you never slip into old patterns

It means you own your part the moment you see it.

It sounds like:

- "I reacted too quickly—let me reset."
- "I misread that. Can we start over?"
- "My emotional horizon was low. That wasn't fair."
- "I thought this was about you, but I see it was about me."

This is not weakness; it is maturity.

MOVING FROM ASSUMPTION

There was a time I misinterpreted someone's silence as frustration with me. I tensed up, mentally preparing to 'fix' whatever problem I assumed existed.

But instead of reacting, I paused.

I asked, **"You've been quiet. What's going on?"**

He exhaled and answered, **"I'm overwhelmed—not with you, just with life."**

Instantly, everything eased up.

Old me would've reacted; new me understood.

And that was the moment clarity replaced assumption—and connection replaced conflict.

AN IMPROVED YOU IS INSIDE — EVEN IF YOU DON'T FEEL LIKE THEM YET

Somewhere inside you, a deeper version is emerging:

More grounded.
More patient.
More clear.
More self-aware.
More intentional.
More emotionally intelligent.

You may not fully *feel* like that person yet—but every moment of clarity pulls you closer.

Identity is built through repetition and self-understanding is built through reflection.

So the turning point comes not when you've mastered perspective, but when you finally decide you want to—and you choose to walk toward it.

This is the moment your story changes—not because everything around you shifted, but because you did.

LEGACY ISN'T GLAMOROUS

How Small Choices Become the Structure of a Life

Legacy is a word people usually attach to money, achievements, or public recognition. But that's not what legacy really is.

Legacy isn't built in grand gestures, public moments, or impressive milestones. It is built in unseen places—in quiet decisions, unnoticed sacrifices, and private standards you hold when nobody else is watching.

Legacy is **who you become** through the things no one applauds.

It is:

- the character you practice when you're tired
- the honesty you uphold when lying would be easier
- the patience you reach for when frustration feels justified
- the follow-through you show when no one would blame you for cutting corners
- the kindness you give when it isn't returned
- the integrity you maintain when the room is empty

Legacy is not a public performance.

Legacy is private architecture.

It's the framing, not the finish work.
The foundation, not the paint color.
The underpinning, not the decoration.
The structure of the edifice, not the height of it.

It's what your life is really made of.

WHAT YOU BUILD IN SILENCE SHAPES WHO YOU ARE IN THE OPEN

In construction, the parts of a house that matter most are the ones most people never see:

- footings
- rebar
- the concrete slab
- hidden beams
- trusses
- structural anchors
- framing
- bracing
- barriers that protect from moisture and stress

From the outside, all people notice is the paint, the finishes, the style. But without the hidden structure, everything eventually collapses.

Legacy works the same way.

Most people only see:

- your achievements
- your confidence
- your talents
- your reputation
- your roles
- your visible success

But what holds all of that together are the unseen parts:

- your private discipline
- your unseen resilience
- your internal alignment
- your quiet decisions
- your unspoken moral code
- your character under pressure
- your willingness to do what's right when wrong is easier

Legacy is the result of what you build silently.

THE NOBODY-IS-WATCHING MOMENTS

There's a moment on every job when nobody's around. The inspector has come and gone, the homeowners aren't there, and your team isn't hovering. There's no one to evaluate your work, checking your quality, or watch your decisions.

And you're left alone with a simple choice:

Do I do what's right or what's easy?

That's the real architecture of legacy.

Legacy is built when:

- you straighten the line no one else will see
- you redo something that technically passed but isn't your best
- you take responsibility when you could quietly shift blame
- you stay honest when dishonesty would go unnoticed
- you give integrity your full commitment even when there's no visible reward

Legacy is not built in crowds. Legacy is built when no one's clapping.

THE LASER

Years ago, we were framing interior walls on a property. One wall kept looking just a little off—not leaning enough to fail, but enough that something in us knew it wasn't right.

The homeowner would've never noticed.
The inspector would've passed it.
It would've disappeared behind drywall and paint.

But we noticed. So, I grabbed the laser to check alignment. When we shot the line, it was barely off—maybe an inch. The kind of thing that would vanish once the house was finished.

One of the guys sighed and said, "No one is ever going to know, Dustin."

I smiled and said, "I'll know. And so will you."

He nodded, tore the wall apart, and rebuilt it until the laser hit dead center.

No homeowner ever thanked us for that wall.

No one celebrated the extra time.

No one even knew.

But, inside us, something became stronger—the commitment to build the kind of work and life we could respect.

That moment taught me:

Legacy is built through standards, not applause.

Through alignment, not attention.

Through choices, not chances.

Legacy is not what people say about you. Legacy is how deeply you respect the person in the mirror.

THE INNER ARCHITECT: WHO YOU ARE WHEN YOU'RE ALONE

Every person has an "inner architect"—the deeper part of you that designs the direction of your life. Most people let that architect operate on autopilot.

They:

- react instead of design
- drift instead of build
- hope instead of choose
- follow emotion instead of principle

Legacy builders live differently.

They intentionally build:

- identity
- character
- emotional strength
- integrity
- reliability
- perspective

- wisdom
- emotional regulation
- compassion

These are not traits you're born with. They're beams you choose—or choose not—to install. You're either choosing to give your inner architect the reins or choosing to build intentionally.

LEGACY IS BUILT IN SMALL, UNSEEN DECISIONS

We underestimate how powerful small private decisions are.

Your legacy is not shaped by your biggest accomplishment.

It's shaped by:

- the tone you use when no one else would call you out
- the temptations you resist that no one would know about
- the shortcuts you refuse that others would've taken
- the effort you give when the reward is invisible
- the respect you show when the other person doesn't 'deserve' it
- the responsibilities you honor when you're exhausted
- the emotional discipline you practice when someone else loses theirs

Legacy is **always** in the small choices.

Character is not something you declare; **it's something you demonstrate.**

THE SHIFTED FOUNDATION

There was a builder who rushed through foundation prep. The grade was slightly uneven and the soil wasn't fully compacted. The footings weren't set as deep as they should have been.

It passed inspection.
It saved time.
It looked fine.

A few years later, the homeowner started noticing:

- small cracks in the drywall
- doors that didn't close quite right
- floors dipping slightly

Nothing catastrophic.
Nothing dramatic.
Just a slow warping of the structure as the foundation settled unevenly.

"I didn't think it would matter," the builder revealed when he was confronted.

But it did.

Everything built on top of a compromised foundation eventually shows the cost. In life, the same is true.

In the long-run:

- small lies become big mistrust
- small compromises become major regrets
- small shortcuts become repeated patterns
- small dishonors become fractured identity

Unseen cracks eventually show up through visible consequences—just not immediately.

Legacy doesn't demand perfection. **But it does demand deeper foundations.**

THE POWER OF HIDDEN ALIGNMENT

In construction, there's a concept called *hidden alignment*—the way things line up beneath the surface:

- beams
- studs
- piping
- wiring
- ducts
- connectors
- anchors

If those aren't aligned, the finish work becomes a nightmare.

Trim doesn't sit right.
Drywall humps.
Cabinets aren't flush.
Doors don't close smoothly.
Floors creak.
Everything feels just slightly off.

Alignment is invisible—until it isn't. People are the same way.

When you align your:

- values
- emotions
- perspective
- actions
- principles
- decisions

You realize everything above the surface flows more smoothly.

Less conflict.
Less chaos.
Less confusion.
Less reactivity.
Less regret.

Hidden alignment produces visible peace.

Legacy Isn't About Success — It's About Structure

Eventually, legacy isn't:

- how much money you made
- how many projects you built
- how many people knew your name
- how impressive your achievements were

Legacy is:

- how well you loved the people closest to you
- how much integrity you walked with

- how consistently you showed up
- how deeply people trusted you
- how safe people felt around you
- how honestly you handled your mistakes
- how respectfully you treated others
- how steady you were under pressure
- how faithfully you kept your commitments

Success fades; legacy remains.

Legacy is not the building—**it's the framing beneath it.**

THE TEST OF LEGACY: HOW DO PEOPLE FEEL AROUND YOU?

People rarely remember your exact words. What they won't forget is the atmosphere you created.

They remember whether they felt:

Safe.
Seen.
Understood.
Respected.
Valued.
Heard.
Supported.
Encouraged.

Or:

Judged.
Dismissed.
Misunderstood.
Unimportant.
Unworthy.
Invisible.

Your emotional presence—the climate you bring into a room—is the real architecture of your legacy.

How you make people feel becomes the story they tell about you long after you're gone.

LEGACY REQUIRES LONG-GAME THINKING

Legacy builders think differently.

They don't ask:

- "What feels good right now?"
- "What's easiest?"
- "What makes me look good?"
- "What gets the fastest payoff?"

They ask:

- "What will matter in five years?"
- "What will I be proud of later?"
- "What builds long-term trust?"
- "What strengthens my future?"
- "What reflects the best version of me?"

Shortcuts create instability simply because circumstances never remain the same—they always change.

The long game, however, builds strength.

THE UNIQUENESS OF YOUR LEGACY

Your legacy isn't supposed to look like anyone else's.

Some people build legacies of compassion.
Some of resilience.
Some of leadership.
Some of trust.
Some of creativity.
Some of service.
Some of honesty.
Some of peace.

Your legacy is the unique synergy of:

- your strengths
- your character
- your experiences
- your decisions
- your values
- your perspective
- your presence

Legacy isn't a monument. **It's a pattern.**

And only you can build yours.

THE THREE QUESTIONS OF LIFE-LONG LEGACY

These questions help you design the structure instead of drifting into it:

1. What do I want people to experience through me?

Peace?
Strength?
Clarity?
Encouragement?
Safety?
Hope?
Wisdom?

Write it down. Then, build toward it.

2. Where am I cutting corners privately?

Not to shame yourself—but to free yourself.

Coming face-to-face with those aspects where you take shortcuts strengthens your resolve to choose 'right' over 'easy.' It helps you confront those fixed reactions and think beyond the present, whether your actions are acknowledged by others or not.

Integrity requires awareness and legacy requires alignment.

3. What part of my life needs a deeper foundation?

Is it:

- honesty?
- patience?
- communication?
- emotional discipline?
- follow-through?
- relationship repair?
- boundaries?
- self-respect?

Just as roots determine fruit, foundations determine structure.

LEGACY IS BUILT DAILY, NOT EVENTUALLY

You don't 'arrive' at legacy. You **build** it—one small choice at a time.

Every time you choose:

- integrity over ease
- honesty over avoidance
- patience over reaction
- understanding over assumption
- generosity over judgment
- consistency over convenience

You're strengthening the structure of your life.

And one day, without realizing it, you'll look around and see:

You didn't just build a life. **You built a legacy.**

Not by performing for others or impressing anyone, but by living with the kind of quiet integrity that only you—and God—ever fully saw.

That is the architecture of legacy.

HIDDEN BEAMS AND QUIET BUILDERS

The Unseen Strengths That Hold You Together When Life Gets Heavy

Some of the strongest structures in the world are held up by beams no one ever sees.

If you've ever walked through a framed home, you know the look: crisscrossed wood, angled supports, temporary braces, long runs of lumber standing tall in a skeleton of future rooms. It doesn't look beautiful or impressive. It doesn't even look intentional at first glance. But those hidden beams are doing more work than anything that will ever be seen on the surface.

Once the drywall goes up, once the paint smooths everything out, once the trim and baseboards make it all look finished, the beams disappear. But they don't become less important just because they're invisible.

If anything, the more invisible they are, **the more important they become.**

Human lives work the same way.

Every person has hidden beams—quiet choices, private standards, internal commitments, invisible disciplines—that hold up the structure of who they are.

And the people who build the strongest lives aren't the ones who shine brightest in public. They're the ones who build the deepest, truest beams in private.

This chapter is about that hidden work—and the quiet builders who rarely get credit, rarely get recognition, rarely get applause... yet carry more weight than anyone realizes.

THE UNSEEN WORK MATTERS MORE

There are two kinds of work in life:

1. Public Work

The visible accomplishments.
The projects.
The results.
The deliverables.
The moments people notice and praise.

2. Inner Work

The emotional discipline.
The patience no one acknowledges.
The restraint no one applauds.
The forgiveness you give silently.
The integrity you walk in privately.
The character you choose in solitude.

Most of the world focuses on public work, but lives are truly built by **inner** work.

If you've ever met someone whose presence feels calm, strong, and grounded, you can trust one thing:

They've done invisible work you'll never fully know.

Because:

- Emotional steadiness is not natural—it's practiced.
- Patience is not effortless—it's cultivated.
- Wisdom is not automatic—it's built through years of internal construction.

The people who seem 'naturally' grounded simply built better beams. It takes work but everyone can do it.

THE QUIET BUILDER

Years ago, I worked with a framer named Steve.

He wasn't loud or flashy. He didn't argue, show off, or need credit. But his work spoke loudly.

Every cut was exact,
Every stud was straight.
Every joint was flush.
Every measurement spot-on.
Every beam aligned.

He wasn't the fastest or the most charismatic. Clients rarely remembered his name.

But every superintendent, every foreman, and every contractor hoped Steve was assigned to their job.

Why?

Because everyone knew:

"If Steve framed it, the rest of the build will be easy."

One day I told him, "You're one of the best I've ever seen. How'd you learn to be so good?"

He just shrugged.

"I don't rush," he said quietly. "And I don't cut corners."

He ran his hand along a perfectly framed wall.

"People won't see this later," he added. "But the house will feel it."

That line stayed with me:

People won't see this later. But the house will feel it.

So will your life.

THE HIDDEN BEAMS IN YOUR LIFE

There are beams in your life right now—invisible supports under everything you do—whether you've noticed them or not.

Some beams are strong.

Some are cracked.

Some need reinforcement.

Some need replacing.

Some you didn't know existed.

Some you've been carrying alone for far too long.

Let's look at a few of the most important ones.

1. THE BEAM OF SELF-RESPECT

Self-respect is the internal standard that shapes every decision, every relationship, and every boundary you hold.

It's quiet. It doesn't show up as arrogance or ego.

Self-respect simply sounds like:

"I know my worth.
I know my values.
I know who I am.
I know what I won't compromise."

When this beam is strong:

- You don't beg for validation.
- You don't tolerate disrespect.
- You don't shrink to make others comfortable.
- You don't abandon your truth for acceptance.

When this beam is weak:

- You question yourself constantly.
- You over-explain and over-apologize.
- You let people take more than you can give.
- You lose yourself trying to keep others happy.

You don't strengthen self-respect in public.

You strengthen it in private in moments when:

- you walk away from what isn't aligned
- you say "no" for the first time
- you honor a boundary no one else will protect

- you choose honesty with yourself
- you refuse to settle

Self-respect is a hidden beam—but it holds up everything.

2. THE BEAM OF EMOTIONAL INTEGRITY

Emotional integrity is telling yourself the truth even when it's uncomfortable.

It sounds like:

- "I'm tired."
- "I'm overwhelmed."
- "I'm triggered."
- "I'm avoiding something important."
- "I'm acting from fear right now."

Most people ignore their emotional truth because it's easier to stay busy than to be honest. But the truth is, whatever you refuse to feel becomes a crack in the structure.

- Suppressed anger becomes resentment.
- Avoided sadness becomes emotional numbness.
- Ignored stress becomes reactive behavior.
- Unspoken fears become controlling tendencies.

Emotional integrity is quiet self-honesty.

No applause. No spotlight. Just alignment.

When this beam is strong:

- You communicate more clearly.
- You express your needs honestly.
- You regulate your reactions better.
- You understand your triggers.
- You see situations more accurately.

Emotional integrity doesn't make you perfect. It makes you **real**—and real is stable.

3. THE BEAM OF FOLLOW-THROUGH

Follow-through is one of the rarest strengths in the world.

For many people, follow-through is conditional. It's something they only do if:

- they feel like it
- they're motivated
- nothing goes wrong
- no distractions show up

But strong lives are built by people who follow-through *even without* immediate payoff. Follow-through is character in motion.

It is:

- finishing what matters
- honoring your word when no one checks
- keeping commitments that won't benefit you today
- doing what's right without needing recognition

This beam is the bridge between who you say you are and who you actually are.

4. THE BEAM OF PERSPECTIVE

Perspective becomes a structural beam when it stops being something you 'remember to use' and starts being something you naturally reach for.

When perspective is in place:

- you interpret more accurately
- you respond more calmly
- you recover more quickly
- you see more clearly

Perspective protects you from:

- emotional distortion
- misread intentions
- unnecessary conflict
- false assumptions
- reactive decisions

When perspective becomes a beam, it doesn't erase emotion—it stabilizes
it.

THE COST OF HIDDEN CORNER-CUTTING

Everyone knows cutting hidden corners on a job seems harmless... until
it isn't. Cut enough corners, and a structure fails from the inside out.

The same is true for people.

Cut these corners often enough and:

- you stop telling yourself the truth
- you start acting from insecurity
- you stop trusting your own decisions
- you become emotionally unstable
- you attract relationships that match your cracks
- you become shaky under pressure

Private compromise becomes public instability. But private integrity
becomes public strength.

THE QUIET BUILDERS YOU NEVER NOTICE

The strongest people in your life are not always the loudest.

They're the quiet builders:

- the friend who listens without needing the spotlight
- the partner who carries emotional weight without complaint
- the coworker who steadies the team without being asked
- the parent who keeps showing up, day after day
- the leader who stays calm when tensions rise
- the person who owns their mistakes before anyone calls them out

These people carry hidden beams.

They are the reason relationships stay healthy.
The reason teams stay grounded.
The reason conflict doesn't explode.
The reason families feel safe.

They're the quiet builders—the ones holding up more than anyone realizes.

The Moment You Realize You're Also a Quiet Builder

At some point—maybe sooner than you think—you'll discover something:

You are becoming the quiet builder in someone else's life.

Someone will lean on your steadiness.
Someone will feel safe because of your clarity.
Someone will grow because of your patience.
Someone will feel understood because of your perspective.
Someone will trust you because your presence calms them.
Someone will raise their standards after watching your integrity.

This is the highest form of leadership—not titles, not status, not power.

It is quiet, grounded influence. A life that stabilizes others because you've learned how to stabilize yourself.

THE THREE QUESTIONS OF THE QUIET BUILDER

To build stronger hidden beams, ask yourself:

1. What internal structure am I strengthening right now?

Is it patience?
Integrity?
Self-respect?
Perspective?
Emotional steadiness?

2. Where am I quietly cutting corners instead of building strong beams?

This realization helps you realign yourself.

3. What version of me will benefit from this work later?

Your future self is depending on the beams you're building today.

YOU ARE BUILDING A STORY — NOT JUST A LIFE

Every choice you make is shaping a narrative. One day, people won't remember most of what you did.

But they will remember:

- how safe they felt with you
- how steady you were under pressure
- how you treated them when they were vulnerable
- how honest you were when no one would've known otherwise
- how your presence gave them room to grow
- how your integrity influenced their own

Your story won't be told through trophies.

It will be told through **beams**:

The quiet, hidden ones.
The ones that required discipline.
The ones that required humility.
The ones that required character.

The Best Part: Hidden Beams Never Go To Waste

Nothing you build privately is ever wasted.

Not one moment of patience, disclipline, honesty, restraint, forgiveness, emotional self-control, or perspective. Every hidden beam strengthens the structure of your life—and the lives that rest on yours.

Someday, someone will walk through the 'finished house' of your life—the person you've become—and they'll feel something different.

They won't know why, but you will.

You'll know it was the beams.

The ones you built quietly.

The ones no one saw.

The ones that held everything together.

This is the work that shapes your story. The work that builds your legacy and creates a life worth living.

THE DAILY BUILD

Tiny Disciplines That Reinforce Identity, Character, and Direction

Most people overestimate the power of big moments and underestimate the power of small ones. They assume life is shaped by major choices—the turning points, the dramatic events, the life-changing opportunities.

But life is shaped far more by the tiny, unseen choices you make every day.

The Daily Build is the quiet truth that who you're becoming is determined not by *occasional* intention, but by *consistent* habits. Not by promises, but by patterns. Not by inspiration, but by repetition. When someone becomes wise, grounded, steady, patient, emotionally strong, and deeply capable, it never happens suddenly.

It happens **brick by brick, day by day.**

The Daily Build is about those small, steady choices that accumulate into who you are.

You don't rise to the level of your goals. **You fall to the level of your patterns.** And you become the sum of your daily decisions.

THE MYTH OF THE GRAND TRANFORMATION

There are wishful stories people love to tell themselves.

Things like:

- "One day I'll change."
- "One day I'll start."
- "One day I'll be better."
- "One day I'll slow down."

- "One day I'll stop reacting."
- "One day I'll finally feel steady."

But "one day" is a myth.

No one becomes patient in a moment. They become patient through a thousand pauses.

No one becomes wise in an instant. They become wise through a thousand choices to listen instead of react.

No one becomes grounded overnight. They become grounded through repeated decisions to stay centered under pressure.

People don't transform because they *want* to. They transform because they *practice*.

That practice is the Daily Build.

THE CONSTRUCTION PARALLEL: SMALL THINGS BECOME BIG THINGS

On a jobsite, the big moments are exciting:

- the first wall stands
- the roof trusses go up
- the windows arrive
- the exterior takes shape
- the cabinets go in
- the carpet is installed

But the real progress happens in the small, ordinary steps:

- a stud placed perfectly straight
- a joint sealed correctly
- insulation tucked neatly
- wiring run properly
- fasteners installed correctly
- measurements taken precisely
- surfaces prepared thoroughly

Miss enough small details and the whole project becomes chaos. Honor the small details and the entire build moves smoothly and becomes a beauty to behold. Life is exactly the same.

Success is rarely one big thing. It's the accumulated weight of **small things done consistently.**

The Power Of Daily Decisions

The real building blocks of your life are things like:

- the tone you choose in a moment of irritation
- the patience you practice when you could rush
- the honesty you offer when lying would go unnoticed
- the effort you give when no one else is watching
- the boundaries you reinforce gently but firmly
- the perspective you choose when your emotions narrow
- the compassion you show to someone who is struggling
- the responsibility you take before you're blamed
- the gratitude you express in ordinary moments

None of these decisions make headlines. None of them draw applause.

But collectively, they build the person you are becoming.

The Daily Build is the architecture of identity.

THE COMPOUND EFFECT OF SMALL HABITS

The Daily Build works like compound interest.

A single day doesn't change much.

A single decision feels small.

A single moment rarely feels transformative.

But compound enough small choices and everything changes.

- 1% more patience a day becomes emotional strength
- 1% more clarity a day becomes wisdom
- 1% more kindness a day becomes a loving presence
- 1% more honesty a day becomes integrity
- 1% more awareness a day becomes maturity
- 1% more steadiness a day becomes leadership

People underestimate the power of consistency. However, consistency is the real architect of strength.

THE HABIT OF PERSPECTIVE

Perspective isn't something you 'learn once.'

You learn it, practice it, apply it, and grow in it daily. Perspective becomes a habit when you:

- pause before defending yourself
- assume positive intent when you're unsure
- listen before forming an interpretation
- communicate instead of guessing
- check your emotional horizon before reacting
- ask clarifying questions instead of assuming
- choose generosity in your interpretations
- let people explain themselves before deciding what they meant

Practice these long enough and your relational world changes.

You stop living in emotional fog.
You stop misreading people.
You stop creating unnecessary conflict.
You stop being ruled by old triggers.

Perspective shifts from a tool you remember occasionally to a lens you live in naturally.

The Dangers Of Neglecting The Daily Buid

Neglect is rarely dramatic.

It's subtle.
It's slow.
It's quiet.
It's comfortable.
It's convenient.

Neglect chooses ease today and cost tomorrow.

Here's the truth most people avoid:

- No one destroys their life in one decision. They erode it through thousands of small choices that weaken their structure.
- No one loses a relationship in a single argument. They lose it through a thousand small dismissals, avoidances, and misinterpretations.
- No one ruins their self-respect in one mistake. They ruin it through repeated compromises they tell themselves 'don't really matter.'

The Daily Build works both ways—you're either building or dismantling.

There is no neutral. No middleground.

THE BUILDER WHO DIDN'T SEE IT HAPPENING

I once walked a jobsite with a builder who couldn't understand why his projects were always behind, chaotic, and stressful.

"I don't get it," he kept saying. "I work hard."

And he did.

But as we walked, I noticed:

- a slightly crooked stud
- a missing nail
- insulation not quite sealed
- an uneven subfloor
- sloppy cuts
- materials poorly stored
- tools left scattered
- prep work skipped

No single mistake was catastrophic. But collectively, they created constant instability.

Every small oversight multiplied downstream.

Everything took longer.
Everything cost more.
Everything created frustration, tension with clients, and pressure on the crew.

He wasn't failing because of one big issue. He was failing because of dozens of small ones.

Not from lack of effort—but from lack of **daily discipline.**

That's how lives drift too.

Not through one big crisis, but through a thousand small moments we choose not to build intentionally.

THE FIVE DAILY BUILDS THAT CHANGE A LIFE

There are five daily disciplines that reshape identity.

They're not dramatic.
They don't take hours.
But done consistently, they shift the trajectory of your life.

Let's walk through them.

1. THE DAILY PAUSE

The skill of pausing is the foundation of emotional clarity.

When you pause, you:

- prevent unnecessary conflict
- stop emotional momentum
- widen your perspective
- move from reaction to intention
- let your nervous system reset
- give others space to be human

A three-second pause can prevent a three-day argument.
A five-second pause can save a relationship from misunderstanding.
A ten-second pause, repeated daily, can change your character over time.

The daily pause builds strength quietly.

2. THE DAILY REFLECTION

Reflection is not rumination.

Reflection is examining your day with curiosity instead of judgment.

Ask yourself:

- What triggered me today?
- What angle was I seeing from?
- Where did I react instead of respond?
- Where did I communicate clearly?
- Where did I misunderstand someone?
- What did I learn about myself?

Reflection is the architect's walk-through—the inspection that improves the next build.

Unexamined days slowly become unintentional lives.

3. THE DAILY ALIGNMENT

This is where you ask:

"Did my actions today align with who I want to become?"

If not, then:

- What needs to be adjusted?
- What discipline do I need tomorrow?
- What beam needs reinforcement?

Daily alignment prevents long-term drift. It recalibrates your direction so you don't wake up one day as a version of yourself you never meant to become.

4. THE DAILY ACT OF SERVICE

Service doesn't have to be grand.

It might be:

- a kind word
- a thoughtful question
- a supportive text

- a helpful gesture
- a moment of genuine listening
- an unexpected compliment
- a simple check-in

Service shifts your focus from self-centered to others-aware. It strengthens empathy, deepens connection, cultivates humility, and grounds your presence.

The more you serve, the more you grow.

5. THE DAILY HONESTY

Honesty is where real transformation happens.

Not just honesty with others—honesty with yourself.

Ask:

- What am I avoiding?
- What am I pretending not to feel?
- What am I afraid to admit?
- Where am I making excuses?
- What truth am I resisting?
- What responsibility am I minimizing?

Self-honesty can feel uncomfortable. But pain isn't the enemy of growth; avoidance is.

Daily honesty strengthens your internal backbone.

THE DAILY BUILD IN RELATIONSHIPS

The Daily Build doesn't just shape *you*—it shapes your relationships.

Strong connection isn't built by fireworks.

It's built by:

- showing up consistently
- communicating clearly
- listening deeply
- apologizing sincerely

- repairing quickly
- choosing generosity
- assuming good intent
- protecting trust
- staying steady in hard moments

It's never the one big romantic moment or grand gesture that keeps people close. It's the daily ones.

You Become What You Practice

You don't become what you promise, hope, dream about, or wish you were.

You become what you **practice.**

If you practice:

- patience → you become patient
- gratitude → you become peaceful
- honesty → you become trustworthy
- discipline → you become reliable
- perspective → you become wise
- compassion → you become safe
- courage → you become strong

Your identity is sculpted by repetition.

The Daily Build turns behavior into character, and character into identity.

THE QUESTION THAT CHANGES TOMORROW

Ask yourself tonight:

"What small decision can I make tomorrow that my future self will thank me for?"

It might be:

- taking a pause instead of snapping
- giving someone grace instead of judgment

- following through on one promise
- owning a mistake
- choosing clarity over assumption
- sending a text you've been putting off
- repairing a conversation
- stepping back instead of escalating
- aligning one small habit with who you want to become

Small decisions change everything.

The Daily Build isn't glamorous. It isn't dramatic or immediately impressive. But it works.

Small decisions made consistently become large, inevitable transformations.

THE BEAUTY OF THE DAILY BUILD

The best part of the Daily Build is this:

You don't need a perfect plan, you just need a consistent direction.
You don't need massive change, you just need repeated alignment.
You don't need dramatic discipline, you just need quiet commitment.
You don't need overnight transformation, you just need daily intention.

Your life doesn't change all at once. It changes one decision at a time.

And the person you become is built in the small moments you choose with intention when no one is watching.

That is the Daily Build.
That is the architecture of growth.
That is how identity is formed—quietly, consistently, daily.

WHEN THE FRAME SHIFTS

How to Stay Grounded When Life Changes Faster Than You Expected

Every structure, no matter how well designed, eventually faces a moment that tests it.

It might be:

- a windstorm,
- a shift in the soil,
- unexpected pressure,
- sudden weight,
- or years of stress accumulating quietly.

When that happens, the frame of the building moves—sometimes subtly, sometimes dramatically.

The same thing happens in life.

You can have a solid foundation.
You can have strong beams.
You can have a clear blueprint.
You can be consistent with your Daily Build.

And still, one unexpected moment—or a series of small internal shifts—can make you feel like the frame of your life is moving under your feet.

Not failing.
Not collapsing.
Just… shifting.

This chapter is about staying steady when that happens.

Because the strength of your life isn't proved when everything is calm. **It's proved when everything moves.**

LIFE DOESN'T ASK FOR PERMISSION TO MOVE

Life never sends a warning that says, "Hey, tomorrow's going to be a big shift—just so you know."

It doesn't ask if it's a good time, wait until you're emotionally ready, or hit pause on your responsibilities.

Life shifts:

- when you're already tired
- when your emotional horizon is narrow
- when your resources are stretched
- when you're mid-build
- when everything feels barely balanced
- when you want change everything but change

And when it does, you can't not feel it. Something in your internal frame starts to move.

Your thoughts wobble.
Your emotions tighten.
Your confidence shakes.
Your plans destabilize.
Your routines get disrupted.
Your clarity fogs.
Your perspective narrows.

You may even feel yourself slipping back into old patterns you thought you outgrew.

This is normal.
It is human.
And, most importantly, it is manageable.

But it requires recognizing the shift early, and remembering who you are even when the ground feels different beneath you.

WHAT SHIFTS, WHAT DOESN'T

When a house shifts because of soil movement, wind, or settling, not everything moves.

Some parts shift.
Some stay locked in.
Some flex.
Some absorb the pressure.
Some need reinforcement.
Some remain completely unaffected.

The structure doesn't collapse simply because it moved. It adapts.

Well, so do you.

When life shifts:

- your circumstances might move—but your character can stay rooted
- your emotions may wobble—but your anchor doesn't have to
- your routines may bend—but your identity can remain steady
- your plans may fall apart—but your purpose can stay intact

The key is learning to stay stable inside yourself while the external frame changes around you.

THE THREE TYPES OF LIFE SHIFTS

Not all shifts feel the same.

Some are sudden.
Some are slow.
Some are internal.

Understanding which kind you're facing helps you respond with clarity instead of confusion.

1. The Sudden Shift

This is the unexpected:

- phone call that changes everything
- job loss
- relationship breakup
- medical scare
- betrayal

- financial blow
- major conflict
- decision someone else made that impacts you

Sudden shifts hit hard and fast. They don't give you time to prepare. Your emotional frame takes the impact all at once.

These shocks are disorienting—but they can also be clarifying. They reveal what's built strongly and what needs reinforcement.

2. The Slow Shift

Slow shifts feel different. You barely notice them… until you do.

They build through:

- ongoing stress
- a gradual drift in a relationship
- a creeping sense of burnout
- weeks of unmet needs
- months of small disappointments
- years of quiet resentment
- long-term neglect of your inner world

Slow shifts sneak up on you.

You hear yourself saying:

- "I don't know when this started."
- "I didn't realize how much this was affecting me."
- "I thought I was fine, but I'm not."
- "I guess it built up more than I realized."

Slow shifts move internal beams quietly until one day something feels off—not shattered, just misaligned.

That misalignment matters.

3. The Internal Shift

Internal shifts are the most personal. They're not caused by events or other people, but by who you're becoming.

Internal shifts happen when:

- you outgrow old patterns
- your perspective changes
- your emotional needs evolve
- your self-respect strengthens
- you gain new clarity
- you realize what you can no longer accept
- you see yourself differently than before

They sound like:

- "I'm changing."
- "I don't want to go backward."
- "I'm ready for something more aligned."
- "I don't respond the way I used to."
- "I need something different now."

Internal shifts signal **growth**, not loss.

When the inside of you expands, the outside of your life has to adjust. And that adjustment can feel like a frame shift.

THE PROBLEM ISN'T THE SHIFT — IT'S THE SURPRISE

People don't panic because life moves. They panic because movement feels out of their control.

Most people don't fear change; they fear instability. They don't fear transition; they fear not knowing what comes next.

The frame shift itself is rarely the real danger. It's the emotional uncertainty that unnerves us.

You can't always control the shifts. But this doesn't imply hopelessness because you can learn how to stay steady in them.

Rule 1: Don't Overinterpret the Moment

When something shifts in your life, your first instinct may be to:

- catastrophize

- assume the worst
- fill in the gaps with fear
- relive old stories
- jump to conclusions
- react impulsively
- retreat inward
- get defensive

But movement does not equal collapse. A shifting frame is not a falling frame.

- Just because something changed doesn't mean it's broken.
- Just because you feel off balance doesn't mean you're unsafe.
- Just because the plan changed doesn't mean your future is ruined.

The first rule of staying steady is:

Don't let fear define the meaning of the moment.

Let perspective catch up before you decide what this shift means.

The first minutes (or days) of a shift are important—not because they decide the outcome, but because they influence your response and your response means everything to your future.

Rule 2: Find Your Internal Anchors

When a frame shifts, builders rely on anchors—structural elements that hold the building steady even when the environment moves. People need these anchors too.

Your anchors might be:

- your core values
- your principles
- your spiritual foundation
- your priorities
- your identity
- your long-term vision
- your character commitments
- your emotional disciplines

- your relational clarity
- your faith
- your sense of purpose

Anchors keep you from being swept away by emotion.

They remind you:

"This moment is temporary; who I am is not."

Anchors don't remove or end the shift. They keep you from losing yourself inside it.

Rule 3: Adjust Without Abandoning Yourself

When life shifts, your instinct might be to:

- overcorrect
- change everything at once
- cut people off
- shut down emotionally
- cling to old patterns
- appease everyone
- overexplain
- overcompensate

While they may seem like sure fixes, they are not what you need. In reality, all of these reactions make the shift harder.

When builders encounter a frame shift, they don't bulldoze the structure. They don't tear everything down and start over.

They adjust what needs adjusting—no more, no less.

You can:

- adjust your expectations without abandoning your values
- adjust your plans without abandoning your purpose
- adjust your approach without abandoning your identity
- adjust your emotions without abandoning your truth

Adaptation is strength, not surrender.

Rule 4: Hold Onto Steady People

When the frame moves, steady people become essential.

On a jobsite, when something shifts, everyone looks toward:

- the most experienced workers
- the calmest minds
- the clearest thinkers
- the people who don't panic
- the ones who've seen this before

You need those people in your life too.

Steady people help you:

- regulate your emotions
- widen your perspective
- separate fear from fact
- avoid impulsive decisions
- hold onto what's true
- remember who you are

Steady people don't stop the shift—they help you stay grounded while it settles.

Rule 5: Trust the Process Of Releveling

When a frame shifts, builders use a process called **releveling**.

They don't:

- panic
- rebuild the house from scratch
- declare the project ruined
- throw out the blueprint

They assess the situation by asking questions like:

- "What moved?"
- "By how much?"
- "What caused it?"
- "What needs reinforcement?"
- "What needs adjustment?"

Then they slowly, carefully, and patiently relevel the structure until it's aligned again. Your life works the same way.

When something shifts:

- Don't abandon everything.
- Don't catastrophize.
- Don't assume it is permanent.

Instead, relevel by.

- Adjusting your expectations.
- Reinforcing your values.
- Strengthening your boundaries.
- Deepening your self-care.
- Widening your emotional horizon.
- Revisiting your priorities.
- Clarifying your relationships.
- Rebuilding what needs attention.

Releveling isn't a step backward. It's a step into new stability.

WHAT FRAME SHIFTS REVEAL ABOUT YOU

Life shifts don't just shake you—they reveal. And they don't just reveal things to you, they reveal things about you.

They show you:

- what you've strengthened
- what you've outgrown
- what you've neglected
- what you've been avoiding
- what you've been pretending was fine
- what you actually value
- where your emotional limits are
- where your internal beams need reinforcement

Shifts reveal truth—not to expose you, but to expand you.

You can't grow without friction.
You can't strengthen without pressure.
You can't deepen without challenge.

Shifts are not punishments. They are invitations.

THE MOST IMPORTANT TRUTH ABOUT FRAME SHIFTS

You don't need the world to stop moving to stay steady. You just need to stay steady while the world moves.

Strength is not the absence of movement. It is the ability to remain grounded despite movement. A person who is steady only when life is stable is not actually steady—they're just untested.

Real steadiness is proven in motion.
Real character is proven under pressure.
Real perspective is proven in disruption.
Real identity is proven in transition.
Real emotional growth is proven in shifting seasons.

When the frame moves and you stay centered—that's strength.
That's growth.
That's maturity.
That's perspective becoming identity.
That's clarity becoming stability.
That's character becoming anchor.

THE GIFT INSIDE THE SHIFT

Every shift carries a gift. It's not always immediately or through comfort but always eventually.

Shifts give you:

- clarity about what wasn't aligned
- insight into who you're becoming
- awareness of what needs reinforcement
- deeper emotional strength
- refined values

- stronger boundaries
- better relationships
- a clearer sense of self
- greater perspective
- future stability

Shifts don't exist to break you. They exist to build you. They expand your capacity and deepen your understanding of yourself and others.

You do not walk out of a shift the same—and that's the point. Pay attention during the shifts in your life and look for the moments of learning that build you.

THE QUESTION THAT ENABLES GROWTH

In every shift, instead of asking:

- "Why is this happening to me?"
- "What did I do wrong?"
- "When will this be over?"

Ask:

- "What is this moment trying to strengthen in me?"
- "What is being revealed?"
- "What is being reinforced?"
- "What version of me is emerging?"

This doesn't make the shift easy. But it does make it meaningful.

When you ask these growth-enabling questions, shifts move from being disruptions to becoming developments.

YOU CAN STAY STEADY EVEN WHEN THE FRAME SHIFTS

Your stability does not depend on:

- perfect circumstances
- predictable routines
- consistent outcomes

- other people behaving perfectly
- life unfolding according to your plan

Your stability depends on:

- your perspective
- your emotional discipline
- your internal anchors
- your clarity
- your values
- your identity
- your alignment
- your self-understanding

Life will move.
Frames will shift.
Seasons will change.

But **you** can remain steady.

Not because nothing shakes—but because shaking doesn't scare you anymore. Not because you control everything—but because you trust yourself through anything. When the frame shifts, you don't fall apart.

You relevel.
You realign.
You reinforce what matters.
You deepen your roots.
You widen your view.
You steady your breath.
You steady your heart.
You steady your life.

This is how you grow. It is how you rise and become unshakable.

REFRAMING THE PAST

Turning Old Stories Into Sources of Wisdom, Not Weight

The past has a way of sticking to us more tightly than we realize.

Not the facts—those fade.

Not the details—those blur.

Not the exact events—those become stories we retell so often we forget what actually happened.

What sticks is the **angle**.

- The way we interpreted what happened.
- The meaning we assigned to the moment.
- The story we built around it.
- The emotion we attached to it.
- The lesson we told ourselves it taught.
- The belief it planted about life, people, and ourselves.

Most of the time, the past doesn't hurt us because of *what* happened. It hurts us because of **how we learned to see** what happened.

Perspective isn't just about the present—it's also about the past.

If your past was filtered through painful or distorted angles, your future will feel narrower, heavier, and more constrained than it needs to be.

This chapter is about learning to **reframe the past** so you can move forward with clarity, instead of carrying old interpretations that don't belong in the life you're building now.

YOU CAN'T CHANGE THE PAST — BUT YOU CAN CHANGE ITS POWER

When people say, "You can't change the past," they mean the events.

But events are not what hold power over you. Your interpretation holds that power.

You can't change what was said, but you *can* change what it meant.

You can't change what someone did, but you *can* change the story that action wrote inside you.

You can't change who didn't show up, but you *can* change what their absence taught you about your worth.

You can't change the mistakes you made, but you *can* change what you learned from them.

The past is not fixed—because the meaning you give the past is not fixed. And meaning is where healing happens. Not in erasing what was, but in reframing what it now means.

Reframing the past doesn't rewrite history. It rewrites your relationship with it.

THE ANGLE OF A MOMENT SHAPES A LIFETIME

Every past moment has two layers:

1. **The Event:** What happened—factually, externally.
2. **The Angle:** What you believed it meant about:

   - yourself
   - other people
   - safety
   - trust
   - love
   - your worth
   - your identity
   - your abilities
   - your place in the world

The event is often neutral or temporary. But the angle can last **decades**.

For example:

- Event: You made a mistake.
  Angle: "I'm always messing things up."
- Event: Someone broke your trust.
  Angle: "People can't be trusted."
- Event: A relationship ended.
  Angle: "I'm unlovable."
- Event: You were misunderstood.
  Angle: "No one ever understands me."
- Event: Someone didn't choose you.
  Angle: "I'm not enough."

None of those angles are factual truths—but they become the **operating system** of your life until you examine them. That's why reframing matters.

Your future shouldn't be run on outdated interpretations.

The Past Is Not a Fact

It's an Unchecked Story

The moment you revisit the past with perspective, something often becomes clear:

What you believed was "just the way it was," was actually just the way you could **see it back then**.

Most people don't realize they've been:

- living with an outdated interpretation
- carrying inherited beliefs that were never theirs to begin with
- replaying stories shaped by childhood, not current reality
- reacting to old angles with adult consequences
- mistaking emotional memory for truth
- building identity around misunderstandings
- repeating patterns that no longer serve who they are now

The past is not a prison. It's a **narrative**.

And narratives can be rewritten—not through denial, but through deeper understanding.

Reframing the past is one of the most powerful forms of freedom.

THE FRAME YOU WERE GIVEN VS. THE FRAME YOU CHOOSE

Everyone is given an early 'frame'—the lens their childhood, environment, and early relationships taught them to see life through.

But childhood frames are not built for adult lives.

For example:

- If you were raised with constant criticism, you may interpret feedback as attack.
- If you were raised with inconsistency, you may interpret stability as suspicious.
- If you were raised with emotional distance, you may interpret closeness as risk.
- If you were raised with constant conflict, you may interpret calm as boredom.
- If you were raised with chaos, you may interpret peace as unfamiliar.
- If you were raised with unpredictability, you may interpret trust as unrealistic.

Old frames create new misunderstandings.

There is nothing "wrong" with you. Your old frame is simply **outdated**.

Reframing is not a betrayal of your past. It's an acknowledgment that you deserve a better angle now.

You can't always control the frame you were given. But you *can* choose the frame you now live with.

YOU CAN'T HEAL WHAT YOU WON'T NAME

One of the most important steps in reframing is **naming** what the past taught you—not to blame anyone, but to reclaim clarity.

Ask yourself, "What did I learn from that moment that I now need to unlearn?"

Let's walk through a few examples.

- **Old Lesson:**
  "I need to handle everything alone."
  New Reframe:
  "I was alone because the people around me were limited—not because I'm unworthy of support."
- **Old Lesson:**
  "I can't trust people."
  New Reframe:
  "I couldn't trust some people. Others are safe—and I can learn to tell the difference."
- **Old Lesson:**
  "I'm too much."
  New Reframe:
  "The people who said that were overwhelmed by their own limitations, not by my value."
- **Old Lesson:**
  "I should stay quiet if I don't want conflict."
  New Reframe:
  "My voice matters. Healthy relationships can handle honest emotion."
- **Old Lesson:**
  "If I make a mistake, love will be withdrawn."
  New Reframe:
  "Real love doesn't disappear when I'm imperfect."
- **Old Lesson:**
  "I need to earn acceptance."
  New Reframe:
  "I am worthy without performance."

Naming the old lesson is the **demolition**. Reframing the lesson is the **rebuild**.

Interestingly, both are essential for healing.

The Past Is Not Just What Happened — It's What You Still Believe About What Happened

Most people think the past affects them because:

- "It was traumatic."
- "It hurt me."
- "It messed me up."
- "It broke me."

But the real impact of the past is not the event—it's the **belief** the event convinced you to hold.

The event ended, but the belief stayed.

Healing is not primarily about the memory. It's about the **meaning**. Reframe the meaning, and the memory loses its power to define you.

REFRAMING DOESN'T INVALIDATE PAIN — IT REVEALS PURPOSE

Some people resist reframing because it feels like:

- making excuses for others
- minimizing what happened
- denying their pain
- pretending everything is okay
- "letting people off the hook"

But reframing is none of those things.

Reframing simply says, "I won't let outdated pain interpret my present."

Pain deserves acknowledgment. It does not deserve **permanence**. Reframing honors the reality of what happened while freeing you from the **distortion** of what it meant.

It separates:

- regret from identity
- grief from self-worth
- past wounds from present wisdom
- formative experiences from limiting beliefs

Reframing doesn't erase the past. It restores your power in the present.

THE BUILDING ANALOGY: RENOVATING OLD ROOMS

Imagine walking through an older home.

Some rooms are outdated.
Some walls need reinforcement.
Some framing needs correction.
Some areas need to be gutted and rebuilt.

Renovation doesn't destroy the house; it restores it.

Your inner world is the same.

You aren't starting over.
You aren't demolishing everything.
You aren't erasing your story.

You are **renovating** the parts that no longer serve you.

- Some memories need new meaning.
- Some beliefs need new framing.
- Some narratives need updated interpretation.
- Some blueprints need correction.
- Some habits need replacement.

Renovation isn't shame; it's stewardship.

You're rebuilding your inner structure into something stronger, safer, and more aligned with who you are now.

A MOMENT OF REFRAMING THE PAST

Years ago, someone close to me misinterpreted something I said and reacted harshly.

They made assumptions about my intentions.
They projected their fears into the situation.
They lashed out emotionally.

In the past, I would have interpreted that as:

- "I must have done something wrong."
- "I'm being misunderstood again."
- "People don't see who I really am."
- "I'm not good at expressing myself."

But this time, something different happened.

Instead of absorbing the blame, I paused and asked, "What angle am I seeing this from?"

And it hit me:

"This isn't about the present moment. This is about an old version of me interpreting this through old wounds."

Once I saw that, things got clearer. I reframed the experience and told myself, "This isn't evidence that I'm inadequate. This is evidence that their emotional horizon is narrow right now."

The reframing didn't make the conflict pleasant, but it protected my **identity** inside of it.

That's the power of perspective applied to the past. It helps you stand in who you've become instead of collapsing into old stories.

THE FOUR LEVELS OF REFRAMING

Reframing the past isn't a single step—it's a sequence.

LEVEL 1: AWARENESS

"I learned this belief in the past."

LEVEL 2: ACCURACY

"That belief wasn't the full truth."

LEVEL 3: REINTERPRETATION

"There's a healthier way to understand that moment."

LEVEL 4: REPLACEMENT

"I choose this new belief going forward."

Awareness cracks the old frame.

Accuracy loosens it.

Reinterpretation removes it.

And, finally, replacement installs the new one.

THE QUESTIONS THAT HEAL THE PAST

Here are some powerful reframing questions:

1. What angle did I learn back then that I've outgrown now?
2. What was actually happening in that moment—not just what I emotionally assumed?
3. What version of me interpreted that experience originally?
4. What would the wiser, present version of me say to that younger version?
5. What truth was missing when that event happened?
6. What did that moment teach me that I now realize wasn't accurate?
7. How can I reinterpret this with compassion for everyone involved—including myself?

These questions don't erase the past. They open doors that have been stuck for years.

COMPASSION IS THE TOOL THAT UNLOCKS THE REFRAME

Compassion is what makes reframing possible.

Compassion:

softens the interpretation

- widens the angle
- reveals humanity
- allows for context
- makes room for perspective

You cannot reframe the past through judgment. You can only reframe it through **understanding**.

Compassion doesn't excuse behavior, but it explains it. And explanation is what frees you.

Compassion turns painful memories into **teachable** ones.

UPGRADING YOUR INNER BLUEPRINT

As you begin reframing your past, you'll notice something powerful: Your internal blueprint starts to **upgrade**.

You stop:

- assuming the worst
- interpreting through old wounds
- repeating outdated patterns
- reacting from childhood lenses
- carrying beliefs that were never fully true
- reinforcing limiting narratives
- shrinking under old fears

And you start:

- choosing healthier interpretations
- responding instead of reacting
- building clearer relationships
- trusting your capacity to grow
- stepping into your present identity
- creating emotional safety for yourself
- strengthening your boundaries
- living forward instead of backward

This isn't just healing—it's transformation.

THE FINAL SHIFT: BECOMING WHO YOU WERE ALWAYS CAPABLE OF BEING

Reframing the past doesn't create a completely new you. It restores the **you** that pain buried—the real, unique you.

You begin to feel more like yourself, but:

- healthier
- wiser
- steadier
- freer
- clearer
- more grounded
- more compassionate
- more aligned with your values

The real you hasn't disappeared. They've been waiting for you to update the frame.

Reframing doesn't erase the past. It **redeems** it.

It turns:

- pain into purpose
- confusion into clarity
- wounds into wisdom
- old limitations into current strength

And, most importantly, it frees you to live **forward**.

Not defined by what happened.
Not limited by who hurt you.
Not constrained by old stories.
Not trapped in outdated interpretations.

You become the builder of your own meaning—and from that moment on, the future opens in a new way.

THE MAGIC HAPPENS IN THE KITCHEN

Tasting, Adjusting and Responding

Using the kitchen as a living metaphor, this chapter reveals how tiny adjustments—timing, patience, attention, and intention—can completely change an outcome. Just as cooking is less about following a recipe and more about tasting, adjusting, and responding to what's happening in real time, life unfolds the same way.

This chapter shows how:

- Two people can follow the same "recipe" and still end up with different results.
- Pressure and stress reveal what's already inside us.
- Patience isn't passive but essential to depth and clarity.
- Awareness and adjustment matter more than perfection.
- Perspective turns ordinary moments into powerful teachers.

More than a reflection on cooking, this chapter invites readers to notice where they rush, assume, overreact, or ignore small signals—and how those habits shape relationships, communication, and emotional outcomes.

It reminds us that growth doesn't come from overhauls—it comes from presence. From noticing. From adjusting just enough, at the right moment, to change everything that follows.

THE SMALL STIR THAT CHANGES EVERYTHING

I've always loved to cook.
Not because I'm a chef or I'm fancy.

But because the kitchen teaches perspective in a way few other places can.

Cooking looks simple from the outside: Ingredients → heat → food.

But the more time you spend in a kitchen, the more you learn something else:

Small things change everything.

A few degrees.
A pinch too much.
A minute too long.
A flavor added at the wrong time.
A stir too early.
A stir too late.

In themselves, these things are not dramatic. There is nothing catastrophic about them. But they are the tiny choices that shift the entire outcome.

And that's when I realized: **Life works the same way.**

The First Lesson: You Can Follow the Same Recipe And Get Different Results

Two people can cook from the same recipe and end up with completely different dishes.

Why?

Because recipes aren't the whole story. **Interpretation is.**

One person tastes as they go; another rushes.
One watches the heat; another assumes it's "fine."
One adjusts; another reacts.
One stays present; another gets distracted.

Same ingredients. Same steps. Different outcomes.

Just like in life.

Two people can experience the same moment—the same conversation, the same words, the same tone—and walk away with opposite reactions simply because:

Perspective is the seasoning that changes everything.

The Second Lesson: Heat Reveals What's Really Inside

Heat doesn't create flavor; it brings out what's already there.

It asks you immediately:

Did you season right?

Did you prepare well?
Did you rush?
Did you overlook something?
Did you assume instead of intentionally choosing?

Stress or pressure constitutes life's 'heat' and it works just like heat works in the kitchen.

Pressure reveals our inner ingredients: our fears, habits, assumptions, interpretations, and emotional reflexes.

Not to blame or shame us—but to show us what needs to be adjusted.

Perspective is the tool that lets you taste your life honestly.

The Third Lesson: Patience is Part Of the Process

Anyone who loves to cook knows this truth:

Some dishes only work if you don't rush them.

You can't crank the heat to force flavor.

You can't hurry tenderness.

You can't bake at double the temperature to save half the time.

Life works the same way.

You can't rush healing.

You can't rush maturity.

You can't rush clarity.

You can't rush relationships into depth.

You can't rush emotional growth.

The timing matters.
The pacing matters.
Your presence matters.

Patience is not waiting—it's allowing the process to unfold correctly.

The Fourth Lesson: Tasting As You Go Is Perspective In Action

Great cooks don't assume. They check, taste, and adjust—as many times as required.
They don't get offended if the dish needs more salt.
They don't take it personally if they added too much spice.
They don't insist the flavor "should be fine" based on the recipe alone.

They stay curious, not defensive.

Imagine if we did that in life. We'd be asking questions like:

"What am I missing?"
"What needs adjusting?"
"Is this reaction accurate?"
"Am I adding too much intensity here?"
"Do I need more softness?"
"Is this moment calling for patience or action?"

Perspective is simply the art of *checking the flavor before serving the reaction.*

The Fifth Lesson: The Best Meals Are Made For Other People

Cooking is rarely about the cook.

It's about the table.
The gathering.
The connection.
The experience everyone shares together.

You don't cook well because you need praise. You cook well because you care about the people eating.

Perspective works the same way.

When you see someone clearly, interpret them generously, and respond with steadiness—the relationship becomes the meal.

Communication becomes connection.

Conversations feel safer.

People open up more freely.

Everyone brings their best.

Perspective makes relationships taste better.

The Sixth Lesson: The Kitchen Reveals Who You Are When Things Go Wrong

Every cook has moments where things go sideways.

Times when:

The sauce breaks.

The steak overcooks.

The bread burns.

You drop something.

You forget something.

You misread the instructions.

In those moments, you can react, panic, get frustrated, blame the oven, blame someone else, or even throw it all out.

Or you can choose to breathe, adjust, pivot, improvise, start again, and learn something.

The kitchen quietly teaches the same truth found in every chapter of this book:

Mistakes don't define you. Your interpretation of the mistakes does.

Great cooks grow through mistakes. Great people grow the same way.

THE REAL SECRET: COOKING IS JUST PERSPECTIVE PRACTICE

Maybe that's why the kitchen feels sacred to me.

It's a place where patience, clarity, interpretation, small choices, presence, heat, generosity, connection and perspective all matter.

Everything you practice here builds emotional strength out there.

Cooking is simply perspective in physical form.

THE INVITATION: FIND YOUR 'KITCHEN'

It may not be cooking for you.
Maybe it's woodworking.
Maybe it's gardening.
Maybe it's music.
Maybe it's painting.
Maybe it's building.
Maybe it's running.
Maybe it's conversation.
Maybe it's parenting.
Maybe it's your morning routine.

But everyone needs a "kitchen"—a place where life slows down and perspective becomes visible.

A place where you learn how to respond, not react.

A place where you learn how small things shape big outcomes.

A place where meaning hides in the ordinary.

A place where you practice seeing life through gentler eyes.

Because the more clearly you see here, the more deliberately you live everywhere.

CHAPTER 24

SEEING THE SACRED IN THE ORDINARY

Training Your Mind to Notice the Daily Miracles Most People Miss

Life is made of small moments.

Tiny, ordinary, forgettable, and overlooked ones.

But here's the underrated truth: The quality of your life is determined by how you see the moments most people miss.

A lot of people are waiting for something big to finally give their life meaning:

A breakthrough.
A promotion.
A dream realized.
A perfect relationship.
A powerful experience.
A major achievement.
A moment of clarity so strong it rewrites everything.

But meaning rarely arrives through big moments.

Meaning usually arrives quietly—hidden inside the ordinary corners of your life.

It shows up in:

- the way you wake up in the morning
- the way you speak to the people you love
- the way you breathe during stress
- the way you notice what others overlook
- the way you respond to daily struggles
- the way you choose gratitude in simplicity

    the way you treat people who can't give you anything
    the way you appreciate what's right in front of you

The sacred is not found only in the extraordinary. The sacred is found in giving **ordinary moments** extraordinary attention.

This chapter is about learning to see life through new eyes—not because life changes, but because *you* do.

MEANING ISN'T A DISCOVERY — IT'S A PRACTICE

Most people think meaning is something you stumble into—something reserved for special days, big events, or dramatic seasons.

But meaning is not found. Meaning is **made**.

And making meaning is simpler than one might expect. You elevate whatever you consistently pay attention to.

- What you notice shapes your experience.
- What you appreciate shapes your emotions.
- What you slow down for shapes your memories.
- What you treat as sacred shapes your identity.

The person who finds meaning in small things lives a richer life than the person waiting for big things. This is why perspective matters so deeply.

When you learn to see clearly, you begin to notice things most people walk right past. And that ability subtly changes everything.

THE MOMENT YOU REALIZE LIFE IS HAPPENING IN-BETWEEN THINGS

Many people assume life happens:

- on vacations
- on weekends
- during milestones
- on holidays
- at celebrations

- when something new begins
- when something exciting arrives

But the truth is:

Life is happening on random Tuesday afternoons.
In conversations over kitchen counters.
In car rides to school or work.
In the text that says, *"Did you make it home?"*
In the quiet after a long day.
In small moments of courage.
In overlooked acts of love.
In silent decisions made alone.
In inside jokes that wouldn't make sense to anyone else.

Life isn't contained in the big events. Life is tucked inside the moments too ordinary to post, too small to celebrate, too quiet to remember—unless you're paying attention.

Seeing the sacred in the ordinary begins when you realize how rare and extraordinary the 'normal' really is.

MAKING THE INVISIBLE VISIBLE

Most people don't lack blessings; they lack awareness.

They don't lack joy; they lack attention.

They don't lack meaning; they lack the perspective to recognize it.

Perspective isn't just a communication tool—it's a spiritual one.

- Perspective reveals what is already in front of you.
- Perspective makes invisible gifts visible.
- Perspective turns routine into significance.
- Perspective transforms the familiar into the meaningful.

When you see differently, you live differently. And the clearer your lens, the more sacred the simple things become.

THE FAVORITE MOMENT I ALMOST MISSED

There was a morning—long before life sped up, before bigger responsibilities, before more complicated seasons—when everything looked simple on the outside but felt rushed on the inside.

I was heading out the door, already halfway into my day in my mind. I was already thinking about the jobsite. The tasks. The schedule. The problems I needed to solve.

As I walked past our small kitchen table, one of my kids looked up at me with a sleepy smile and asked, "Are you going to give me a hug before you go?"

No one else remembers that moment.
It wasn't photographed.
It wasn't remarkable by any normal standard.
It wasn't important on a calendar.

But it was sacred.

Something in me slowed down. I stopped, turned around, knelt down, and hugged them longer than usual. I felt small arms wrap around my neck. Maybe six seconds passed.

But something inside me shifted:

This is life. Right here. This.

This is what I will miss someday if I'm not careful.

Meaning didn't arrive in some dramatic revelation. It arrived in a quiet invitation I almost walked past.

Ordinary seconds become sacred the moment you pay attention to them.

The Problem Isn't a Lack Of Beauty — It's a Lack Of Presence

People say things like:

"Life is boring."
"Life feels repetitive."
"Life is just the same thing every day."
"Nothing special is happening."

The issue is rarely life itself. The issue is the **lens**.

Beauty is everywhere—but distraction blinds us.

Joy is available—but stress drowns it out.

Connection is present—but haste dulls it.

Sacredness is woven into daily life—but many are waiting for fireworks.

Presence is the only requirement for beauty. If you want to see the sacred, you have to be present enough to notice the ordinary.

THE DAILY MOMENTS MOST PEOPLE WALK PAST

These are the moments people overlook every single day—the ones quietly shaping their emotional life:

- The moment sunlight hits your window.
- The quiet ride to work or school.
- The sound of someone laughing in the other room.
- The feeling of a warm shower after a long day.
- A deep breath that actually fills your lungs.
- The smell of food cooking in the kitchen.
- A conversation that didn't turn into conflict.
- Someone remembering something small about you.
- A simple text from someone you care about.
- Being able to solve a problem you once felt powerless against.
- The comfort of familiar places and routines.
- The luxury of a normal, uneventful day.

Most people walk right past these moments without realizing that these are the moments that build a life worth living.

Meaning doesn't hide in the rare, dramatic, or spectacular. It hides in the 'nothing special' that is, in reality, everything.

ORDINARY MOMENTS MATTER BECAUSE THEY ARE HONEST

The ordinary is honest.

There's no performance in daily moments. No need to impress or any stage to stand on. No spotlight. No audience.

Ordinary moments reveal your truest self:

- Who you are at home.
- Who you are when no one is watching.
- Who you are after a long day.
- Who you are when you're tired.
- Who you are when you're relaxed enough to drop your guard.

Big moments show who people *want* to be. Small moments show who they *really* are.

Learning to see the sacred in those small, honest moments helps you become someone who doesn't miss the best parts of their own life.

THE SECRET OF GRATITUDE: NOT AN EMOTION, BUT A SKILL

Most people treat gratitude like a feeling that shows up when life is good.

But gratitude is less of an emotion and more of a **skill.** When practiced consistently, it becomes a reflex.

Gratitude isn't pretending everything is fine. It's noticing what's good—especially when it would be easier to overlook it.

Think of it like adjusting the brightness on a camera: change the focus, and the whole picture shifts.

Gratitude turns:

- inconvenience into patience
- routine into blessing
- effort into meaning
- interruptions into opportunities
- simplicity into abundance

You stop needing extraordinary experiences to feel joy. The ordinary becomes enough. And when the ordinary is enough, you live a richer life than most people ever realize is possible.

The Practice Of Awareness

If you want to elevate the ordinary into something sacred, start here:

Once a day—literally once—pause and ask, "What is beautiful about this moment?"

It might be:

- The way your child's voice sounds down the hall.
- The comfort of familiar routines.
- The quietness of early morning.
- The steadiness of your own breath.
- The softness in someone's eyes when they look at you.
- The safety of your home.
- The warmth of being hugged.
- The peace of closing your eyes after a long day.
- The simple privilege of being alive right now.

This practice takes ten seconds. But over time, what it does to your heart is profound.

You begin to see life as it actually is—not as your stress, fear, or hurry interprets it.

THE MOST UNDERRATED SKILL: SAVORING

Savoring is the ability to let a good moment land.

It's not nostalgia.
It's not longing for the past.
It's not wishing life were different.

Savoring is simple: You let a good moment be fully good.

You pause.
You notice.
You breathe.

You let yourself feel it.
You don't minimize it.
You don't rush it.
You don't scroll past it.

Savoring turns a two-second moment into a two-minute memory.

It is a skill that:

- deepens joy
- strengthens gratitude
- protects you from emotional burnout
- widens your emotional horizon
- reinforces your identity as someone who fully experiences life

Savoring is how ordinary moments become sacred ones.

THE SACRED ISN'T JUST 'SPIRITUAL' — IT'S 'SIGNIFICANT'

When people hear 'sacred,' they often think 'religion,' 'ritual,' or 'mystical.'

But sacred simply means: Set apart and given weight. Recognized as meaningful.

You can treat almost anything as sacred:

- a quiet morning
- a warm meal
- a genuine conversation
- a moment of laughter
- time with someone you love
- a slow walk at sunset
- the feeling of being safe
- the stillness before sleep
- the breath you didn't realize you were holding

Sacredness isn't about making life dramatic. It's about treating real life as **significant**.

When you give ordinary moments sacred attention, you start living a fuller, deeper, more meaningful life—without changing your circumstances at all.

THE GIFT INSIDE THE ORDINARY

The ordinary offers you:

- peace
- grounding
- emotional balance
- connection
- presence
- gratitude
- perspective
- calm
- enjoyment
- fulfillment
- clarity
- comfort
- stability

The ordinary doesn't demand anything from you.
It doesn't try to impress.
It doesn't overwhelm.

It simply waits to be noticed.

The ordinary is generous. It's constantly offering you more life than you realize you're walking past.

THE FINAL SHIFT: THE WORLD HASN'T CHANGED — YOUR EYES HAVE

When you start seeing the sacred in the ordinary, something subtle but powerful happens:

The world doesn't suddenly look different. *You* do.

- Your heart is softer.

- Your mind is quieter.
- Your emotions are steadier.
- Your relationships are deeper.
- Your gratitude is easier.
- Your stress is lighter.
- Your perspective is wider.
- Your presence is stronger.
- Your days feel fuller.

You realize you were never waiting for meaning. You were surrounded by it.

All you needed were the eyes to see it.

"That Was the Good Stuff."

At some point, everyone looks back on a season of life and realizes:

"That was the good stuff."

Not the vacations.
Not the bigger paychecks.
Not the awards or milestones.

But:

- the breakfasts together
- the shared laughter
- the car rides
- the ordinary dinners
- the slow weekends
- the quiet evenings
- the unremarkable conversations
- the comforting routines
- the small acts of kindness
- the simple togetherness

The sacred was always there. You just didn't know to call it that yet.

This is your invitation to recognize it **now.**

Not later.

Not "when things calm down."

Not when you finally feel caught up.

Not when life feels easier.

Now.

"Why the urgency?" you might be asking.

It's because the ordinary moments you're living today are the sacred memories you'll ache for tomorrow unless you see them for what they truly are while you still have the chance.

So, why waste another second?

BECOMING UNSHAKABLE

The Practice of Emotional Levelness

There's a certain kind of person you meet who stands out—not because they're loud, impressive, or have everything figured out.

They stand out because they're **steady**. Calm. Composed. Unshaken by what shakes everyone else.

These people carry themselves with a quiet internal levelness, as if the world can storm around them and something in them still stays anchored. You feel safer around them. You think more clearly in their presence. You become calmer just by being near them.

This chapter is about becoming that person.

Not perfect.
Not emotionally numb.
Not detached.

Just **level**.

- Level enough that life doesn't knock you off-center every time it moves.
- Level enough that you don't rise and fall with every shift in someone else's mood.
- Level enough that conflict doesn't consume you.
- Level enough that stress doesn't distort you.
- Level enough that unpredictability doesn't unbalance you.

The world is unpredictable.
People are unpredictable.
Circumstances are unpredictable.

But **you** can remain level.

And when you do, everything in your life—your relationships, your inner peace, your decision-making, your emotional well-being—begins to change.

THE SECRET OF LEVEL PEOPLE

People who seem level aren't lucky. They're not born with rare emotional DNA. They didn't just "come out that way."

They're **practiced**.

Level people have learned how to:

- pause when others react
- see clearly when others get clouded
- regulate their emotions in real time
- stay grounded through discomfort
- widen their perspective automatically
- hold their identity steady when others crumble
- respond with intention instead of impulse

These are not personality traits. They are **skills.** And that means they are totally trainable, learnable, and buildable.

So you can become one of these people too.

The world doesn't need more intensity, more reactivity, more volatility, or more emotional chaos. The world needs more levelness.

Your home needs it.
Your relationships need it.
Your work needs it.
Your future needs it.
You need it.

Staying level is not about being calm. It's about being **clear**.

WHY LEVELNESS MATTER MORE THAN CONFIDENCE

Most people chase **confidence**.

They want to feel powerful, capable, certain. But confidence is episodic. It rises when things are going well and falls when they're not.

It depends on:

* circumstances being favorable
* emotions being stable
* situations feeling manageable

Levelness is different.

It is:

* reliable
* consistent
* steady
* independent of circumstance

Confidence says, "I can handle this."

Levelness says, "Even if I can't, I know how to stay steady."

Confidence requires strength; levelness requires **perspective**.

Confidence fluctuates; levelness anchors.

Confidence depends on performance; levelness depends on **clarity**.

If you must choose—choose levelness.

Confidence may **impress** people. Levelness **grounds** you and helps people feel grounded in the calm energy you give off.

THE STRUCTURAL ANALOGY: WHY LEVELNESS MATTERS IN BUILDING AND IN LIFE

In construction, levelness is everything. If the floor isn't level, nothing else sits right.

In a building where the floor isn't level:

* Cabinets install crooked.

- Doors don't close correctly.
- Floors creak.
- Walls crack over time.
- Furniture wobbles.
- Finish work becomes a nightmare.

A house that isn't level might look fine on the surface—for a while. But the problems always show up later. Life works the same way.

If your internal world isn't level:

- your relationships wobble
- your decisions tilt toward emotion instead of clarity
- your boundaries bend under pressure
- your stress cracks your patience
- your communication angles toward misunderstanding
- your reactions become unbalanced
- your peace becomes unstable

Internal levelness determines external stability.

You can't build a steady life from an unsteady heart.

THE FIVE SOURCES OF INTERNAL LEVELNESS

If you want to stay level, you have to know what throws you off.

Most instability comes from one of five destabilizers:

1. **Emotional Overload:** Too many emotions stacked with no processing. Your emotional backpack is full and you're still adding weight.
2. **Unclear Boundaries:** Letting other people's moods, expectations, or reactions control your internal state.
3. **Misinterpretation:** Reading meaning where there is none. Assuming, predicting, guessing, instead of clarifying.
4. **Ego Interference:** Protecting your pride instead of your peace. Needing to be right more than you need to understand.
5. **Unresolved Past:** Old wounds distorting new moments. Yesterday's pain interpreting today's interactions.

Level people don't avoid these forces. They **recognize** them.

They don't just react. They *diagnose* before they respond.

THE FIRST SKILL OF LEVELNESS: EMOTIONAL REGULATION

Emotional regulation is not suppression. It's not pretending you don't feel. It's not putting on a strong face while everything burns inside.

Emotional regulation is the ability to **feel fully** without reacting impulsively.

Think of it like a dam:

- A bad dam blocks water until pressure builds and it bursts.
- A healthy dam channels water and controls the flow.

Regulation doesn't stop emotion; it **directs** it.

Level people do three simple things:

1. **They label their emotions accurately.**
   "I'm anxious."
   "I'm overwhelmed."
   "I'm disappointed."
   "I'm embarrassed."
   "I'm hurt."
   Naming the emotion reduces its power.
2. They separate emotion from truth.
   "This is how I feel—that doesn't automatically make it reality."
3. They pause before expressing anything.
   Even a three-second pause gives clarity time to catch up.

Regulation is the foundation of levelness. You cannot stay level if you don't regulate emotion.

THE SECOND SKILL: PERSPECTIVE WIDENING

Life feels chaotic when your perspective narrows.

When you emotionally zoom in:

- everything feels personal
- everything feels urgent

- everything feels threatening
- everything feels overwhelming

Widening perspective calms your nervous system.

Level people ask:

- "What else could this mean?"
- "What version of me is reacting right now?"
- "Will this matter in a week? A year?"
- "Is this a fact or a feeling?"
- "Beyond the tone, what is the intention behind this?"
- "How would I see this if I wasn't stressed?"

When you back up mentally, situations look different. Perspective widens. Intensity drops.

THE THIRD SKILL: DETACHING FROM MOMENTS

Unleveled thinking sounds like:

- "I failed, therefore I *am* a failure."
- "They're upset, therefore I *did* something wrong."
- "This went badly, therefore I'm not enough."

Level people separate their feelings from who they are because they understand that:

- Moment ≠ Identity
- Mistake ≠ Character
- Someone's reaction ≠ Your worth
- Conflict ≠ Relationship failure
- Emotion ≠ Reality

This separation is massive. It allows you to remain steady even when a situation is chaotic.

With it, life can move—and you still stay level. But without it, every bad moment becomes a verdict about who you are.

THE FOURTH SKILL: INTERNAL BOUNDARIES

While external boundaries protect your **time, space, and energy**, internal boundaries protect your **thoughts, emotions, and peace**.

Internal boundaries sound like:

- "I won't take this personally."
- "I don't have to solve this right now."
- "Their tone is about them, not me."
- "I refuse to argue from pure emotion."
- "I will not abandon myself to keep the peace."
- "I can pause before responding."

Without internal boundaries, you become emotionally porous. Everything gets in and destabilizes you.

Levelness requires an internal 'frame' that doesn't move every time someone else does.

THE FIFTH SKILL: DECISION-MAKING FROM A PLACE OF SELF-RESPECT

Unleveled decisions are driven by:

- guilt
- fear
- impulse
- insecurity
- pressure
- other people's expectations
- emotional discomfort

Level decisions are driven by:

- values
- clarity
- alignment
- long-term consequences
- emotional neutrality

- identity
- self-respect

Self-respect is the compass of levelness. When you honor and respect who you are and who you're becoming, your decisions stop destabilizing you.

Levelness is maintained not by being calm, but by being **self-aligned**.

WHAT THROWS YOU OFF-LEVEL THE FASTEST?

Everyone has 'destabilizing triggers'—moments that shake their internal levelness the quickest.

Common ones include:

- being misunderstood
- feeling disrespected
- being ignored
- being blindsided by conflict
- feeling unappreciated
- being criticized
- feeling out of control
- experiencing uncertainty
- seeing someone else's anger
- feeling abandoned or dismissed

Your job isn't to eliminate these; it's to **understand** them. Once you know your destabilizers, you can prepare for them.

Preparation builds steadiness.

THE THREE PHASES OF STAYING LEVEL

Staying level isn't one thing.

It's three phases you move through again and again.

PHASE 1: PRE-LEVELING (BEFORE THE STORM)

This is the preparation work you do daily:

- your routines
- your emotional hygiene
- your thought patterns
- your boundaries
- your sleep and rest
- your self-respect
- your internal dialogue
- your perspective practices

You don't build stability *in* the storm. You build it **before** the storm so you can use it when it hits.

PHASE 2: MID-LEVELING (IN THE MOMENT)

This is what you do when life actually shifts:

- you pause
- you breathe deeply
- you name your emotion
- you widen your perspective
- you refuse to assign instant meaning
- you choose curiosity over defensiveness
- you separate the moment from your identity
- you remember your long-game vision
- you ask clarifying questions instead of assuming

Mid-leveling is where you apply what you've built. It doesn't stop hard moments from happening—but it keeps them from owning you.

PHASE 3: POST-LEVELING (AFTER THE MOMENT)

This is the reflection you do afterward:

- What threw me off?
- Where did I misinterpret?
- What part of me was reacting?

- What did I learn about myself?
- What would the steady version of me do next time?
- What needs reinforcement in my internal structure?

Post-leveling is how you upgrade your emotional architecture.

Each reflection turns one moment into long-term growth.

THE ROLE OF SELF-KINDNESS IN STAYING LEVEL

People assume levelness requires toughness. But real levelness requires **gentleness**.

Shame is one of the fastest ways to destabilize yourself.

You cannot stay level if you:

- constantly criticize yourself
- punish yourself for being human
- replay every mistake as proof you're failing

Self-kindness is not weakness; it's emotional alignment.

It sounds like:

- "I had a moment—now I'm recovering."
- "I'm learning, not failing."
- "I can repair this."
- "I needed a pause; that's okay."
- "I'm trying, and that matters."

Compassion steadies the heart, bit criticism shakes it.

WHEN STAYING LEVEL MATTERS MOST

Staying level matters most:

- when others lose their temper
- when someone misinterprets you
- when conflict surfaces
- when you're tired
- when you're anxious

- when your past gets triggered
- when things go wrong unexpectedly
- when someone else's emotions spill onto you
- when your plans collapse
- when your identity feels tested

Anyone can stay level in calm water.

Your true structure isn't revealed until you're in rough water.

THE MOMENT YOU BECOME THE STEADY ONE

There will be a day when you notice something:

You've become the level person others rely on.

Not because you're perfect.
Not because you don't feel.
Not because you never wobble.

But because you know how to **steady yourself**.

People will:

- lean on your steadiness
- trust your presence
- calm down around you
- open up to you
- ask for your perspective

You will become a grounding presence in the room.

And you'll realize something important:

You don't just stay level for others—you stay level for **you**.

Your peace becomes a priority.
Your clarity becomes a lifestyle.
Your steadiness becomes part of your identity.

That's emotional maturity.

The Final Shift: Stability As a Way Of Being

This is when staying level stops being something you 'try' to do. It becomes who you are.

You:

- interpret more accurately
- take things less personally
- let emotions rise and fall without panicking
- remain calm in hard conversations
- speak from clarity instead of fear
- listen with curiosity instead of defense
- act from alignment instead of pressure
- maintain boundaries without guilt
- repair quickly when things wobble
- trust yourself to navigate hard moments

Levelness becomes your emotional home.

You no longer cycle into old patterns.

You no longer allow yourself to be thrown off-balance by every unpleasant situation. You no longer believe every emotional story your mind tells you. You no longer react to other people's instability.

You become **steady**. Not perfectly or flawlessly, but consistently enough that your life feels different.

Staying level is not the absence of storms. It is the presence of **internal anchors**.

THE WORLD IS UNPREDICTABLE — BUT YOU DON'T HAVE TO BE

Unpredictability will always exist.

It's baked into:

- relationships
- work
- parenting

- building a business
- building a life
- managing change
- navigating conflict

growing as a person

You can't control unpredictability. But you can control your **response** to it.

Levelness is that response.

It makes you:

- stronger than uncertainty
- clearer than conflict
- calmer than chaos
- wiser than emotion
- more grounded than disappointment

Levelness is a quiet form of leadership—over yourself first, and then over the spaces you influence.

The unpredictability won't stop. But when you're level inside, you stop being destabilized by it.

You become:

- the steady one
- the grounded one
- the clear one
- the calm one
- the centered one
- the anchored one

This is the power of staying level.
This is the strength you carry forward.
This is who you are becoming.

SIDE QUEST 12: "The Daily Level Practice"

Tagline: Ground yourself before you speak.

Action Steps:

Three times a day:

1. Pause
2. Breathe
3. Ask yourself: "What angle am I seeing this from?"
4. Decide if that angle is true or emotional.

Outcome: Upgraded self-regulation and clarity.

SIDE QUEST 13: "The Five Small Repairs"

Tagline: Tiny reinforcements prevent big collapses.

Action Steps:

1. Choose 5 tiny repairs to make this week:

   - A message you owe someone
   - Cleaning up a small mess
   - Completing a task you've delayed
   - Re-centering a relationship
   - Fixing something emotional or practical in your life

   Each repair strengthens your identity.

Outcome: A restored sense of competence and internal stability.

SIDE QUEST 14: "The Long View Journal"

Tagline: Choose who you're becoming, not just how you feel now.

Action Steps:

Each evening answer:

1. "Where did I act from the short view today?"
2. "Where did I choose the long view?"
3. "What long-view decision do I need to make tomorrow?"

Outcome: Improved long-term thinking and reduced emotional reactivity.

THE LONG VIEW AND THE SHORT VIEW

Mastering the Two Lenses That Shape Every Choice

Every decision you make is influenced by one of two perspectives:

The Short View

or,

The Long View.

These two lenses shape:

- how you respond
- how you interpret
- what you prioritize
- what you fear
- what you pursue
- what you ignore
- what you protect
- what you sacrifice

The **Short View** is your immediate lens—the **now**.
The **Long View** is your future lens—the **later**.

Both lenses matter.
Both are necessary.
Both have value.

But **how** you use them determines the trajectory of your life.

This bonus chapter is about using these two lenses on purpose— so you stop making decisions that cost you later and start making decisions that create a life you're proud of.

WHY MOST PEOPLE LIVE IN THE SHORT VIEW

Most people default to the Short View because the Short View is:

- emotional
- urgent
- reactive
- charged
- immediate
- instinctive
- grounded in self-protection
- driven by comfort
- shaped by old habits
- influenced by fear

The Short View asks:

- "How do I feel right now?"
- "What's easiest in this moment?"
- "What gets rid of this discomfort?"
- "What gives me relief?"
- "What avoids conflict?"
- "What calms this anxiety?"
- "What feels good right here?"

The Short View is powerful—and dangerous—because it makes sense *right now*… but often costs you **later**.

The Short View tends to choose:

- avoidance over honesty
- comfort over growth
- reaction over clarity
- impulse over intention
- relief over responsibility
- emotional charge over emotional maturity

Most people don't realize they're living inside the Short View. Their life is shaped by **right-now thinking**:

- right-now emotions

- right-now frustrations
- right-now desires
- right-now pain
- right-now fears

Life becomes stronger, clearer, and more aligned the moment you begin seeing through the Long View.

THE LONG VIEW: THE LENS OF FUTURE STRENGTH

The Long View asks completely different questions:

- "Who am I becoming?"
- "How will this decision age?"
- "What does this mean for the future me?"
- "What matters five years from now?"
- "What choice honors my character?"
- "What aligns with my values?"
- "What leads toward my vision?"

The Long View isn't dramatic.

It's steady. Calm. Rooted. Patient.

The Long View thinks in terms of:

- legacy
- consequences
- identity
- alignment
- emotional maturity
- resilience
- growth
- long-term fulfillment

The Short View asks, "What do I want?"

The Long View asks, "What will I be proud of?"

The Short View reacts.
The Long View responds.

The Short View protects the moment.
The Long View protects the future.

The Short View satisfies the impulse.
The Long View strengthens the character.

Once you learn to switch between these lenses, your entire life begins to shift.

THE TENSION BETWEEN THE TWO VIEWS

Every meaningful decision holds a quiet tension:

- the comfort of **now** vs. the strength of **later**
- the relief of **avoiding** vs. the peace of **addressing**
- the ease of **staying the same** vs. the benefit of **growing**
- the short-term **emotion** vs. the long-term **identity**

Most regrets are born from Short View decisions made in emotionally narrow moments just as most moments of deep pride are born from Long View decisions made in clarity.

All transformation happens when the **Long View** becomes stronger than the **Short View**.

The Short View is Reactive — The Long View is Creative

When you live in the Short View, you are always reacting:

- to stress
- to people
- to pressure
- to emotion
- to discomfort
- to fear

When you live in the Long View, you are creating:

- your future
- your stability
- your character

- your relationships
- your boundaries
- your emotional strength
- your identity

Short View = survival.
Long View = growth.

Short View = protecting the moment.
Long View = shaping the life.

You need both—but not equally.

The Long View must **lead** the Short View, not the other way around.

The Short View Makes Small Problems Feel Big

The Long View Makes Big Problems Feel Small

When you're stuck in the Short View:

- a tone feels like an attack
- a misunderstanding feels like rejection
- a conflict feels like disaster
- a mistake feels like failure
- discomfort feels like danger
- uncertainty feels like threat

When you step into the Long View:

- conflict becomes growth
- discomfort becomes training
- setbacks become redirection
- mistakes become strategy
- misunderstandings become opportunities
- waiting becomes preparation

The Long View doesn't erase difficulty—it **resizes** it.

Short View = **magnification**.
Long View = **perspective**.

THE PERSON YOU ARE NOW CAN SABOTAGE THE PERSON YOU'RE BECOMING

Here's the real war inside every choice:

Your current self vs. your future self.

Your current self wants:

- comfort
- ease
- validation
- safety
- escape
- relief
- sameness
- instant gratification

Your future self wants:

- strength
- clarity
- maturity
- capability
- stability
- wisdom
- discipline
- alignment

The Short View serves the **current self**.
The Long View serves the **future self**.

Behind every decision, there is a subtle question:

"Which version of me am I choosing to honor right now?"

THE THREE AREAS WHERE SHORT VIEW ALMOST ALWAYS WINS

(Unless You Intervene) Short View thinking dominates in three key areas:

1. Conflict

Short View wants to:

- defend
- prove
- react
- withdraw
- argue
- protect pride

Long View wants to:

- understand
- clarify
- repair
- communicate
- preserve connection
- prioritize the relationship over the moment

If the Short View wins, you damage trust.
If the Long View leads, you **strengthen** it.

2. Emotion

Short View listens to the **loudest** feeling while Long View listens to the **deepest** truth.

Short View is urgent; Long View is patient.

Short View says, "Say it now."

Long View says, "Say it right."

3. Identity

Short View acts from insecurity.
Long View acts from integrity.

Short View is about protecting self-image.
Long View is about protecting character.

Short View wants approval.

Long View wants alignment.

You become a stronger person when the Long View guides you through Short View moments.

THE SHIFT HAPPENS IN THE PAUSE

The Short View acts instantly. The Long View activates when you **pause**.

The pause is the bridge between your two selves.
It's the space where perspective catches up.
It's the moment where clarity surfaces.
It's the difference between reaction and wisdom.

In the pause, ask:

- "What does the future me want here?"
- "What decision ages well?"
- "What will I wish I did a week from now?"
- "What honors my values?"
- "What strengthens my identity?"

These questions turn Short View moments into Long View opportunities.

THE LONG VIEW IS BUILT THROUGH REPETITION

You don't become a Long View person in a single breakthrough. You become one through **practice**.

Every day. In small ways.

With choices like:

- pausing before responding
- asking one clarifying question
- taking responsibility early
- repairing quickly
- choosing honesty over ease
- choosing generosity and curiosity over assumption

- choosing patience over urgency
- choosing alignment over impulse

Every Long View choice builds emotional strength.
Every Short View choice creates emotional drift.

The more you practice the Long View, the more natural it becomes—until it begins to feel like instinct.

HOW TO TRAIN YOURSELF TO SWITCH VIEWS ON COMMAND

Here's the practical framework—how you actually do this in real time.

There are four steps to training the Long View:

STEP 1: NOTICE THE SHORT VIEW MOMENT

Your first signal is **emotional contraction**:

- irritation
- defensiveness
- fear
- urgency
- impulsiveness
- insecurity
- tension

When you feel your internal world tighten, you're in the Short View.

Awareness is half the battle.

STEP 2: NAME THE IMMEDIATE DESIRE

Ask yourself, "What does the Short View want me to do right now?"

It might be to:

- avoid
- lash out
- withdraw
- prove

- blame
- react
- defend
- seek validation

Naming it pulls it out of the dark. What you can name, you can choose not to obey.

STEP 3: ASK THE LONG VIEW QUESTION

Now ask, "What decision honors the future version of me?"

This is where clarity rises above emotion. It is where wisdom beats reaction and identity leads behavior.

STEP 4: TAKE THE LONG VIEW ACTION

This is where growth actually happens.

The Long View action may feel harder in the moment—but it feels better *after* the moment.

Long View choices look like:

- clarifying instead of assuming
- listening instead of reacting
- expressing instead of avoiding
- repairing instead of withdrawing
- responding calmly instead of emotionally
- holding boundaries instead of people-pleasing
- choosing alignment instead of impulse

This is how you become stronger: one Long View decision at a time.

THE MOST POWERFUL PART OF LONG VIEW THINKING

The Long View does something subtle and extraordinary:

It makes you **proud** of yourself.

Not loudly. Not for show. But in a quiet, steady, grounded way.

You begin to feel:

- aligned
- mature
- wise
- capable
- steady
- trustworthy to yourself
- emotionally safe inside your own mind

The Long View builds **self-respect**.
Self-respect builds **identity**.
Identity builds **consistency**.
Consistency builds **stability**.
Stability builds **confidence**.
Confidence builds **calm**.
Calm builds **clarity**.

And clarity builds a life you actually love living.

THE SHORT VIEW COSTS YOU PEACE — THE LONG VIEW CREATES IT

Short View decisions create:

- regret
- conflict
- miscommunication
- emotional chaos
- identity confusion
- instability
- shame
- self-doubt

Long View decisions create:

- peace
- clarity
- emotional strength

- trust
- relational safety
- confidence
- stability
- a life that feels coherent and aligned

Peace is not the absence of difficulty.

Peace is the accumulation of Long View choices.

THE LONG VIEW MAKES YOU UNMISTAKABLY DIFFERENT

As you master Long View thinking, something shifts:

- People start trusting you differently.
- Conflicts resolve faster.
- Relationships feel safer.
- Your emotional world feels calmer.
- Your decisions become clearer.
- Your identity becomes stronger.
- Your days feel more intentional.

You stop living by accident and start living on purpose.

You stop reacting and start leading yourself.

You stop repeating old patterns and start creating new ones.

Transformation becomes sustainable—not because you changed everything in one dramatic moment, but because you changed how you see everything in **every** moment.

THE FINAL TRUTH: THE FUTURE IS BUILT IN MICRO-DECISIONS

Here's the heart of it:

Your future isn't built in big events. It's built in **tiny decisions**, **tiny responses**, **tiny interpretations**.

The Short View makes these moments feel small.
The Long View makes these moments **significant**.

And once you see the significance, you start choosing:

- clarity over emotion
- purpose over impulse
- identity over insecurity

From that point on, every decision becomes a doorway:

- Short View → immediate relief
  Long View → lasting strength
- Short View → emotional reaction
  Long View → emotional maturity
- Short View → protection
  Long View → growth
- Short View → escape
  Long View → clarity
- Short View → survival
  Long View → legacy

Every moment is a chance to choose the version of yourself you're becoming. And when you consistently choose the Long View, you don't just **get through** life—you **build** it.

On purpose.
With perspective.
One decision at a time.

THE COMPANY THAT SHAPES YOUR CLARITY

Why the People Around You Quietly Determine How Clearly You See

There's a truth most people underestimate until life proves it to them:

You don't just *have* a perspective. You *borrow*, *absorb*, and *reinforce* perspective from the people around you.

Whether you realize it or not, the people you live with, work with, spend time with, laugh with, struggle with, and seek counsel from are constantly shaping how you interpret the world.

Not through speeches or advice, but through proximity.

Perspective is contagious. And over time, you become the sum of the perspectives you allow closest to you.

This chapter is about why **who you surround yourself with matters more than most people are willing to admit**—and how the right people can steady you when your clarity wavers.

WHEN YOUR PERSPECTIVE ISN'T ENOUGH

Even the most grounded people have moments when their perspective narrows.

Moments when:

- emotion clouds judgment
- stress distorts interpretation
- frustration tightens the emotional horizon
- hurt makes everything feel personal
- fear whispers stories that sound convincing

No one sees clearly all the time.

Clarity is not a permanent state—it's a practice. And sometimes, maintaining that practice requires help. This is where the right people matter.

When your perspective is off, **you need people who can see what you can't**—not people who simply agree with whatever you're feeling.

The right people don't just validate your emotions. They help you **recalibrate your interpretation**.

You Need People Who Can Hold a Wider Angle Than You

Strong relationships aren't built on constant agreement. They're built on **shared respect and expanded perspective**.

The people who help you grow are often the ones who:

- ask better questions instead of giving quick answers
- challenge your assumptions without attacking your character
- tell you the truth without trying to win
- slow you down when you're emotionally speeding
- remind you who you are when the moment tries to redefine you

They don't collapse your experience; they widen it.

They don't say, "You're wrong."
They say, "Let's look at this from another angle."

And that distinction changes everything.

THE DANGER OF SURROUNDING YOURSELF WITH NARROW PERSPECTIVES

It's easy to surround yourself with people who:

- reinforce your frustrations
- amplify your anger
- validate your resentment
- fuel your worst interpretations
- encourage you to stay stuck

It feels supportive in the moment. But the truth is that it quietly shrinks you.

When everyone around you:

- sees the world as hostile
- interprets everything personally
- blames instead of reflects
- reacts instead of responds

You start doing the same. Not because you want to—but because **perspective spreads**. Over time, you don't just share opinions.

You share emotional habits.

And that shapes who you become.

YOU BECOME THE SUM OF WHO YOU KEEP CLOSE

This isn't motivational language. It's reality.

You become influenced by:

- how your friends interpret conflict
- how your colleagues respond to pressure
- how your family handles disagreement
- how your inner circle talks about people who aren't present

If the people closest to you:

- assume the worst
- avoid responsibility
- stay reactive
- blame others
- resist growth

That environment will eventually pull you in that direction—unless you intentionally and actively choose otherwise.

Perspective doesn't just shape moments. It shapes identity.

THE COURAGE TO LISTEN WHEN YOU DON'T WANT TO

Surrounding yourself with people of good perspective requires humility.

Because it means being willing to hear:

- "You might be missing something."
- "That reaction makes sense—but it might not be the full picture."
- "What if there's another explanation?"
- "How do you want to handle this five years from now?"

That isn't always comfortable. But growth rarely is.

Listening is not weakness. It is **confidence in your ability to learn**.

The people who grow the most aren't the ones who are always right. They're the ones who are willing to be taught.

THE RIGHT PEOPLE STEADY YOU — THEY DON'T CONTROL YOU

Good perspective partners don't tell you what to think. They help you think more clearly.

They don't take your agency; they strengthen it.

They don't make decisions for you; they help you see the decision more accurately.

And when you're surrounded by people like that:

- your reactions soften
- your clarity increases
- your emotional horizon widens
- your choices improve
- your life becomes lighter

Not because life gets easier—but because **you see it more accurately**.

CHOOSING YOUR CIRCLE IS A FORM OF SELF-RESPECT

Who you keep close is not accidental; it's a decision. And it's one of the most important perspective decisions you'll ever make.

Ask yourself:

- Who helps me see clearly?
- Who challenges me respectfully?
- Who widens my perspective instead of narrowing it?
- Who calls me forward instead of keeping me stuck?

Those people are not just companions. They are **stewards of your future clarity**.

THE FINAL TRUTH

You don't grow alone. You grow in environments—emotional, relational, conversational environments.

And when you choose to surround yourself with people who:

- value perspective
- respect truth
- practice humility
- encourage growth
- widen the angle

You give yourself an extraordinary gift:

The ability to see clearly—even when life makes that difficult.

Because sometimes, the clearest perspective you'll ever find is reflected back to you by someone who cares enough to help you see.

Epilogue

Clarity Is a Life You Build

Clarity is not a surge of insight.

It's not a breakthrough moment or a single shift that suddenly makes everything easy.

Clarity is a practice.

A way of moving through the world with intention instead of assumption, awareness instead of reactivity, and perspective instead of emotional fog.

Clarity shows up in the smallest places.

It shows in the way you:

- interpret a tone instead of reacting to it
- pause long enough to let understanding catch up
- choose patience over urgency
- give others the generosity you once withheld from yourself
- slow down enough to see the sacred inside the ordinary
- steady yourself when the frame of life shifts

This book was never meant to be something you *finish*. It was meant to be something you *practice.* Something you return to. Something you build with—one choice, one pause, one interpretation at a time.

Because the truth is simple and life-changing:

Your life strengthens every time you choose clarity over assumption, perspective over reaction, presence over distraction, and understanding over fear.

Those tools you discovered in this book? Carry them with you.

Use them in the conversations that matter.
Use them when life gets loud.
Use them when you feel yourself tightening, shrinking, or slipping into old angles.

Use them when you want to protect your peace without abandoning your heart.

You are building someone new—steadier, clearer, wiser, more grounded, more yourself than ever before. And that process unfolds one clear moment at a time.

Your next chapter literally and metaphorically begins now.

Walk into it with the clarity you've built… and the perspective that will guide you forward.

This book is designed not just to be read—but to be practiced.

Here's how to get the most from it:

1. Read slowly.

Perspective is not absorbed quickly. Pause often. Reflect often.

2. Revisit chapters.

The more you grow, the more you'll see.

3. Complete the workbook.

Don't skip it. Writing reveals truths the mind hides.

4. Apply one concept per week.

Massive change happens through small consistency.

5. Use the Long View.

What matters most is not how you feel today, but who you are becoming tomorrow.

6. Let this book become a reference tool.

Return to it during conflict, confusion, or emotional overwhelm.

Perspective becomes clarity through repetition.

The Practical Toolkit for Clarity, Growth & Daily Application

This workbook is here to help you live what you've read—so perspective becomes a daily practice, not just an idea.

As you work through these pages, you'll be strengthening the seven growth practices:

1.   *Widen your emotional horizon*
2.   *Understand your own reactions*
3.   *Interpret others more generously*
4.   *Stay steady during conflict*
5.   *Strengthen your identity*
6.   *Reframe your past*
7.   *Build a clearer future*

Use this workbook like a training ground:
Write with honesty.
Reflect with curiosity.
Return often—growth deepens with repetition.

SECTION 1 — WIDEN YOUR EMOTIONAL HORIZON

Practice: Noticing When Your Angle Gets Narrow

1. Think of a moment from last week that you misinterpreted at first.

- *What did you assume?*
- *What was actually true?*
- *How might a wider emotional horizon have changed your first interpretation?*

Write here:

____

____

____

____

____

____

____

____

____

____

____

____

____

____

____

____

____

2. Where do you jump to conclusions the fastest?
(Examples: relationships, work, texts, silence, tone, conflict.)

- *Why do you think this pattern exists?*
- *Which emotion narrows your perspective most (stress, fear, insecurity, anger, exhaustion)?*

Write here:

3. What emotional "tightness" tells you your perspective is shrinking?

Tension? Defensiveness? Overthinking? Silence? Control?
List your personal early-warning signs.

Write here:

SECTION 2 — UNDERSTAND YOUR OWN REACTIONS

Practice: Seeing What's Happening Inside You, Not Just Around You

4. Describe the 'steady version' of yourself.

- *How do they carry themselves?*
- *How do they respond to stress?*
- *How do they communicate?*
- *How do they interpret conflict?*
- *Who are they becoming?*

Write here:

____

____

____

____

____

____

____

____

____

____

____

____

____

____

____

____

____

Where do you already feel yourself becoming stronger?

Think small wins: a better pause, a calmer response, a softer tone, a clearer boundary.

Write here:

6. What destabilizes you most quickly—and why?

- *What kinds of moments shake you (being misunderstood, criticized, ignored, surprised, etc.)?*
- *What emotion sits underneath the reaction (fear, shame, uncertainty, old stories)?*

Write here:

SECTION 3 — INTERPRET OTHERS MORE GENEROUSLY

Practice: Moving From Assumption to Curiosity

7. Who in your life deserves more generosity in how you interpret them?

- *What assumptions have you been making?*
- *What might be going on in their world that you don't see?*
- *What curiosity question could you ask instead?*

Write here:

____

____

____

____

____

____

____

____

____

____

____

____

____

____

____

____

____

____

8. Think of a recent moment where you took something personally.

- *What did you assume they meant?*
- *What else could have been true from their angle?*

Write here:

9. What is one conversation you need to repair or reopen—and what's a more generous approach to it?

- *What do you want them to feel in that conversation (safe, heard, understood)?*
- *What perspective questions could you bring?*

Write here:

SECTION 4 — STAY STEADY DURING CONFLICT

Practice: Choosing Clarity Over Reactivity

10. Describe how you typically react when conflict first appears.

- *What happens in your body?*
- *What happens in your thoughts?*
- *What happens in your tone or words?*

Write here:

11. Think of a recent conflict. Break it into the three layers from the book:

- ***Surface issue*** *(What actually happened or was said?)*
- ***Interpretation*** *(What did you believe it meant?)*
- ***Emotional charge*** *(What did it stir up inside you—fear, shame, feeling unseen, pressure, etc.?)*

How might clarity at each layer have changed the conversation?

Write here:

____

____

____

____

____

____

____

____

____

____

____

____

____

____

____

____

____

____

12. If you handled that same conflict again from the Long View, what would you do differently?

- *What would you protect: your pride, or the relationship?*
- *What phrase, question, or pause would help you stay level?*

Write here:

13. Write one 'steady sentence' you can use in your next hard conversation.

(Examples:

"Help me understand what you heard in what I said."

"I want us to understand each other more than I want to be right."

"I need a minute so I can respond clearly, not reactively.")

Your sentence:

Write here:

____

____

____

____

____

____

____

____

____

____

____

____

____

____

____

____

____

____

____

SECTION 5 — STRENGTHEN YOUR IDENTITY

Practice: Becoming the Person You Can Trust

Identity isn't who you say you are—it's who you practice being.

14. What identity trait do you want to embody more fully right now?

Strength? Patience? Confidence? Honesty? Compassion? Calmness? Clarity?

- *Why this one?*
- *Where do you already see traces of it?*

Write here:

____

____

____

____

____

____

____

____

____

____

____

____

____

____

____

____

____

15. What small daily action would reinforce that identity trait?

Think tiny and repeatable:

- *A phrase you say to yourself*
- *A question you ask before responding*
- *A boundary you hold*
- *A pause you practice*

Consistency matters more than intensity.

Write here:

16. What behaviors contradict the identity you want to build?

Where does your "default self" pull you off-track?
List them without judgment—this is inspection, not condemnation.

Write here:

17. What is your "Identity Anchor" statement?

A short sentence that reminds you who you're choosing to become.

Examples:

- *"I respond with clarity, not reaction."*
- *"I build trust through consistency."*
- *"I am steady in moments that once shook me."*
- *"I speak honestly and kindly."*

Write yours here:

18. What environment supports your future identity?

- *Who helps you grow?*
- *Who drains you?*
- *Which spaces strengthen you?*
- *Which habits shape your tone, energy, and clarity?*

Write here:

19. How will you measure identity growth over the next 30 days?

It's not perfection but trajectory. What signs of progress will you look for (more pauses, quicker repairs, clearer boundaries, softer tone, etc.)?

Write here:

20. Who will notice your identity growth first—and how?

Often, others feel the shift before we do.

- *Who will sense the difference?*
- *What will they likely experience around you?*

Write here:

SECTION 6 — REFRAME YOUR PAST

Practice: Updating Old Interpretations So They Stop
Running Your Present

21. What old belief from your past feels outdated now?

- *Who or what taught it to you?*
- *Where did it originate (home, school, a relationship, a specific moment)?*
- *Which part of you still holds onto it?*
- *What do you choose to believe now, with clearer perspective?*

Write here:

22. Choose one painful memory and gently reframe it.

- *What new meaning can you give it now?*
- *What truth was missing at the time?*
- *How can you interpret your younger self with more compassion and context?*

Write here:

23. Compare your past self's interpretation with your present self's clarity.

- *What do you understand now that your past self simply couldn't yet?*
- *What does that reveal about how much you've grown?*

Write here:

____

____

____

____

____

____

____

____

____

____

____

____

____

____

____

____

____

____

____

____

*Practice: Daily Patterns, Long View Thinking & Ordinary
Sacred Moments*

24. What is one habit you want to practice every day for the next 30 days?

- *Why this habit now?*
- *How does it support the future you want to build?*

Write here:

25. Identify one unhelpful pattern you want to break this month.

What will you replace it with? (Example: replacing "shutting down" with "asking one clarifying question.")

Write here:

26. List 5–10 micro-decisions your future self will thank you for.

Think small and specific.
(Examples: "Pause before replying when I'm upset," "Clarify instead of assuming," "Repair the conversation sooner.")

Write here.

27. Write a short letter from your future self to your present self.

- *What perspective are they offering?*
- *What do they understand that you don't yet?*
- *What strength are they calling you into?*

Write here:

28. What Long View choice can you make today that slightly shifts your trajectory?

It can be tiny—a repair, a pause, a boundary, a step, a decision.
Intention is what matters.

Write here:

29. List five ordinary moments you want to start noticing more consciously.

Why these?
What quiet meaning do they hold for you?

Write here:

30. What slows you down enough to actually notice life?

A practice? A mindset? A place? A time of day?
How can you build more of that into your week?

Write here:

31. What brings you joy that costs nothing?

These moments reveal what truly matters to you.

Write here:

32. What daily questions will help you stay aligned with the life you're building?

Choose 2–3 to ask at the end of each day.

Examples:

- *"Did I respond like the person I'm becoming?"*
- *"Where did I lose perspective—and why?"*
- *"What am I proud of today?"*
- *"Where can I adjust tomorrow?"*

Write your questions here:

Final reflection

The Last Look Before You Step Forward

Before you close this book and step back into your life, pause for a moment. Not the kind of pause that fills empty space—the kind that invites clarity in.

You've traveled through perspective.
You've learned how interpretation shapes experience.
You've seen how meaning forms inside the angles you choose.
You've discovered how steadiness, clarity, and emotional maturity are built one decision at a time.
You've reexamined your past.
You've reframed your identity.
You've strengthened your choices.
You've moved from reaction to intention.

And now, you stand at the threshold of something powerful:

The ability to see differently—so you can live deliberately.

Growth is not measured by how much you know; it's measured by how differently you choose.

If something inside you feels lighter, clearer, more aware, more grounded—honor that feeling.
It means something shifted in you.
It means your internal architecture is stronger than it was before.
It means you're carrying a new steadiness into your life.
It means you're ready for the next version of yourself.

Take a breath. Settle in. Feel the ground under your feet.

This is your life. Your moment. Your build. And from here onward, you get to choose your angles with intention.

Use these questions for personal reflection, book clubs, teams, or growth groups.

1. Which chapter challenged you the most, and why?

2. Which chapter felt like it described your life exactly?

3. What new perspective helped you interpret someone differently?

4. How has this book changed the way you communicate?

5. What assumption do you want to stop making?

6. What does the 'steady version' of you look like?

7. What moment from your past needs reframing now?

8. What Long View decision are you ready to make?

9. What daily habit from the book do you want to implement first?

10. How can your relationships improve if you bring more clarity and less assumption?

A call to action

What to Do With Your New Clarity

Clarity without action becomes unused potential.

Perspective without practice becomes forgotten insight.

Understanding without integration becomes just another book on a shelf.

So here is your call to action—practical, simple, and doable:

1. Choose one principle to practice this week.

Not all of them. Just **one**.

Maybe it's:

- pausing before reacting
- asking for clarification instead of assuming
- choosing the Long View in a moment of frustration
- interpreting someone else with generosity
- noticing the sacred in the ordinary
- staying level when someone else isn't

Practice it, intentionally, for seven days. Pay attention to what shifts—inside you and around you.

2. Revisit the chapters that spoke the loudest.

Your perspective deepens each time you reread. Your clarity expands and your understanding grows roots.

If a chapter tugged at something inside you, that's your future self tapping your shoulder.

Go back there. There's more to see.

3. Work through the pages that follow.

Write.

Reflect.

Be honest.

Be curious.

Use the workbook questions to strengthen your inner structure.

The more you write, the more you see. And the more you see, the more intentional you become.

4. Enter your next conversation differently.

Bring:

- clarity instead of assumption
- steadiness instead of reactivity
- curiosity instead of defense
- generosity instead of judgment

One conversation can transform a relationship—or quietly begin to restore one.

5. Share this with someone who needs a new angle.

Not because they're broken or because you're "fixing" them.

But because perspective is a gift—and sometimes people just need someone to hand them a different lens.

6. Commit to becoming the most steady, grounded version of yourself.

Not for applause.

Not for validation.

Not for perfection.

But because:

- a steady life is a meaningful one
- a clear life is a powerful one
- a grounded life is a generous one

This is your build now. Your moment to live deliberately. It is where perspective stops being an idea and becomes the way you move through the world.

Your Next Step in the Series

You've widened your perspective, deepened your awareness, strengthened your steadiness, clarified your identity, and learned to interpret moments, people, and yourself with new eyes.

Now comes the shift that matters most: living deliberately with the clarity you've built.

This book gave you the lens.
The next book shows you how to use it.

Your next step is Book 2 in the Perspective Series:

The Choices That Build You: Mastering the Decisions That Shape Your Life. (coming soon)

If this book reshaped how you *see*, the next book reshapes how you *choose*—one decision, one pattern, one moment of intention at a time.

See differently. Live deliberately.

BOOK 1—WHAT YOU MEANT, WHAT I HEARD
Understanding perspective, clarity, and emotional steadiness.

BOOK 2—THE CHOICES THAT BUILD YOU
How strong decisions shape identity, relationships, and a stable life.

BOOK 3—TAKING THE HIGH ROAD
Doing what's right, even when others choose differently.

BOOK 4—POSITIVE IN THE STORM
Choosing optimism, resilience, and strength through every season.

BOOK 5—WHAT MATTERS MOST
Seeing through the noise and building a meaningful life.

THE CHOICES THAT BUILD YOU

How Strong Decisions Shape a Strong Life

If Book 1 taught you how to see clearly, Book 2 will teach you how to *choose clearly.*

- How do you make decisions you're proud of?
- How do you avoid choices that cost you?
- What do strong people decide differently?
- How do you build a life that reflects your values?
- How do you become someone others can trust and depend on?
- How do you choose the high road when the low road looks tempting?

Book 2 will take you deeper into:

- self-discipline
- emotional maturity
- long-term thinking
- boundaries
- courage
- relational wisdom
- identity-aligned living

Clarity shapes your vision while choices shape your life.

Book 2 begins where this one ends—with the choices that define who you become.

www.ingramcontent.com/pod-product-compliance
Lightning Source LLC
Chambersburg PA
CBHW031144160726
47991CB00004B/1555